☆ THE ROCKETS' RED GLARE

THE ROCKETS' RED GLARE

The Maritime Defense of Baltimore in 1814

BY SCOTT S. SHEADS

With a Foreword by Walter Lord

Tidewater Publishers, Centreville, Maryland

Cover: "A View of the Bombardment of Fort McHenry . . ."
Courtesy of The Peale Museum, Baltimore, Maryland

Library of Congress Cataloging in Publication Data

Sheads, Scott S., 1952-
The rockets' red glare.

Bibliography: p.
Includes index.
1. Baltimore, Battle of, 1814. 2. Baltimore (Md.)—
History—War of 1812. I. Title.
E356.B2S54 1986   975.2'603   86-40238
ISBN 0-87033-363-1

Manufactured in the United States of America
First edition

To my uncle LEONARD DANIEL SHEADS
and to the Officers and Crew of the
PRIDE OF BALTIMORE

CONTENTS

☆ ☆ ☆ ☆ ☆ ☆ ☆ ☆ ☆ ☆ ☆

Appendices

FOREWORD

The British attack on Baltimore in 1814 has been so wrapped in the mystique of "The Star-Spangled Banner," it's easy to forget that the battle had an interest and significance of its own.

First was the enormous lift it gave a young and uncertain America. Until Fort McHenry, the War of 1812 had not gone well. Apart from Commodore Perry's victory on Lake Erie and some successful single-ship encounters on the high seas, the American effort was a story of bungled campaigns, disastrous battles, and inept leadership. Dissension was rising.

Then suddenly—only three weeks after the humiliating capture and burning of Washington—came this unexpected victory at Baltimore. Never mind that the British force was not very big; the "conquerors of Napoleon" had been turned back. This glorious event, coupled with the almost simultaneous defeat of another British force at Plattsburg, New York, silenced all voices of doubt and kindled a new burst of patriotism and national pride. It was a spirit that would burn bright through the country's formative years, until the very eve of the Civil War.

More tangible were the effects that the victory at Baltimore had on the peace negotiations currently in progress at Ghent in Belgium. The American and British negotiators had been sparring indecisively since August 1814. When the news of the capture of Washington arrived, the British tone noticeably hardened. But then came word of the American success at Baltimore and Plattsburg, and now it was the Americans' turn to be tough. As the chief British delegate Henry Gilbourn wrote his government, "If we had either burnt Baltimore or held Plattsburg, I believe we should have had peace on the terms which you have sent us in a month at least. As things appear to be going on in America, the result of our negotiation may be very different."

And so it proved. America may not have "won" the War of 1812, but thanks in considerable measure to the triumph at Baltimore, she at least gained a "tie." Everything reverted to the pre-war status quo.

Militarily, the attack on Fort McHenry falls into a class by itself. It marked the only time the system of forts set up to guard America's coast was ever really tested by an invading force of at least some size and strength.

Fourteen warships, boasting a combined firepower of 290 guns, worked their way up the shallow Patapsco River and let fly at the fort from a range of two to three miles. For nearly twenty-four hours they showered the defenders with 1500-1800 shells, bombs, cannonballs, and rockets. There was little pinpoint accuracy, but even today the weapons seem surprisingly powerful. A single British bombship could hurl a 190-pound cast-iron shell two miles. Yet the defenders hung on, and in the end the British fleet retired back down the river, as the garrison raised its famous flag in mocking triumph.

Meanwhile on land the British army had no better luck. With their commander killed in an early skirmish, the troops slowly advanced, till confronted by an unmovable American defense line on the eastern edge of Baltimore City. The enemy force reluctantly returned to their transports.

The American defenders who repulsed both "Nelson's Navy" and the Royal Army regulars merit special attention. They were mostly volunteer sailors and militiamen, and represented an ideal that reached its zenith in this engagement—the concept of the "citizen soldier." The young republic scorned the impressments, conscripts, and mercenaries of the old world. It would defend itself through its own free citizens, who would leave their ploughs and forges to serve their country in its hour of need. Wearing perhaps no more uniform than the garb of their trade, they would rush to the nation's defense, usually serving under their own elected officers. Citizen soldiers and soldier citizens, they were one and the same thing.

The idea was sound only in a simpler world without sophisticated weapons, and even then, poor leaders could bring disaster. The rout of the American defenders of Washington proved that. But it somehow worked at Baltimore, probably due to the fiery leadership of General Sam Smith. The result makes our hearts beat faster, even today.

The military side of this citizen's force is painstakingly pieced together in William Marine's classic, *The British Invasion of Maryland, 1812-1815*. Now Scott Sheads does the same for the maritime side. His rosters include U. S. Navy and Marine regulars as well as many seamen from privateers and merchant ships beached by the British blockade. Some fought in units from their ships, others under the banner of the Marines or the U. S. Sea Fencibles. It is fitting and proper that each man should be individually listed, for that's the way they were regarded at the time. Friends and neighbors, they were heroes all.

WALTER LORD

Acknowledgments

There are a number of individuals and institutions to whom I would like to extend my sincere gratitude for the assistance they have given me in the preparation of this volume.

Foremost is the Fort McHenry National Monument and Historic Shrine of the National Park Service whose excellent photostat archives in the Historical and Archeological Research Project were placed at my disposal. Much of the material for this book was taken from this unsurpassed collection. Special appreciation goes to Superintendent Karen Wade and Chief Ranger Terry M. Dimattio, and to the staff of the library, Darschell D. Washington, Gartner (Lou) Miller, William Justice, and Janet Schwartzberg, andespecially to Historian Paul E. Plamann. I also want to thank William Stokinger, Brooke Blades, and David Orr, National Park Service archeologists, for giving me the benefit of their professional expertise.

I am especially grateful to John H. McGarry III, Registrar at the U. S. Marine Corps Historical Center, and a former colleague, for sharing with me the results of his own study of the Battle of Baltimore.

I am deeply indebted to Richard A. Von Doenhoff, Stuart L. Butler, Michael Music, and Robert Matchette of the National Archives, to Dean Krimmel, Reference Center, The Peale Museum, and to Donna Ellis and Karen Stuart, manuscript librarians at the Maryland Historical Society, who guided me through their excellent collections.

William G. LeFurgy, Baltimore City Archivist, was particularly helpful with material on the Marine Artillery and the Maryland Militia; Ralph Clayton and Robert Gilmore, at the Enoch Pratt Free Library, assisted me on countless occasions in locating Baltimore newspapers.

For special kinds of assistance I am very indebted to the following: Dr. Fred W. Hopkins, Jr., Graduate Dean, University of Baltimore, who provided a much valued critique based on his own vast knowledge and writings on the Chesapeake Campaign and the U. S. Chesapeake Flotilla; Michael Morgan, Frederick C. Maisel III, Hyman Schwartzberg, and Gerald Backof, historian-colleagues, who shared their historical viewpoints and literary insights throughout the project; Leah W. Paslick who spent many hours correcting my initial mistakes (the number of which must have seemed endless); Eleanor Hurley for her unfailing literary assistance; and Captain Ernest W. Peterkin, USN (Ret), whose own extensive military research and friendship enabled me to learn what the phrase "citizen soldier" really means.

Finally, I would like to express special gratitude to my friend Walter Lord, author of the excellent *The Dawn's Early Light* (1972), who provided me with his own extensive research papers, especially Midshipman Robert Barrett's account.

 THE ROCKETS' RED GLARE

INTRODUCTION

The seamen, that exposed, storm-beaten race who convey the riches of commerce with little but of its dangers, with a noble disregard of individual benefit, bestow their labors and offer their lives to protect the community.
>—American & Commercial Daily Advertizer *(Baltimore)*,
>   *April 22, 1813*

Not far from the wharves of Baltimore's maritime birthplace at Fell's Point, there is a small reminder of the city's maritime heritage – the Glendy Graveyard. Here at the corner of Gay and Broadway streets, enclosed within a small wrought iron picket fence, is a headstone weathered by time and neglect. Its inscription, barely discernible, reads simply "George Stiles." This name was well known in Baltimore during the early nineteenth century. Stiles and his compatriots— fellow merchant and sea captain Baptist Mezick; ship chandler James Ramsey; ship prize agent Joel Vickers; and Captain Herman Perry, commander of the privateer *Harrison*—all represented the city's maritime elite when our nation's flag carried fifteen stars and fifteen stripes. These merchantmen-sailors were all members of a naval militia company of masters and mates of vessels who, with their brethren of the maritime trades, were beached by the British naval blockade during the War of 1812.

Nearby is the grave of Reverend John Glendy, for whom this site was later named. Pastor of the Second Presbyterian Church on East Baltimore Street, he later served as Chaplain of the United States Senate in 1815. On a Sunday morning in the summer of 1813, he invited the city of Baltimore's invaluable corps of seamen, known as the First Marine Artillery of the Union and commanded by Captain George Stiles, to receive an address "prepared and suited to the occasion."

They wore no known uniform, but rather the civilian clothing of their respective trades. With them this day were other members of the community—citizen soldiers, as they were known. They now listened with rapt attentiveness to the Reverend Glendy, their orator, as he emphasized "the justice of this war for Free Trade and Sailor's Rights."

The eloquence of this popular naval slogan exceedingly pleased those in attendance. Other maritime soldiers who likely shared the same sentiments included Sea Fencibles, Marines, Navy, and Chesapeake Flotillamen. All of these brave lads of the ocean ashore would soon provide Baltimore with steadfast defiance against Britain's military might.

The War of 1812 against Great Britain had finally and unexpectedly swung southward from the Canadian frontier to the Chesapeake tidewater. A grand offensive was launched under the command of Vice Admiral Sir Alexander Cochrane, newly appointed commander in chief of the North American Station of His Majesty's forces, toward the nation's unprotected capital.

"A View of the Bombardment of Fort McHenry." Courtesy of The Peale Museum, Baltimore, Maryland.

In late August of 1814, a major British expeditionary naval force arrived in the Chesapeake Bay, alarming the inhabitants who resided along the shores of the peaceful tidewater countryside. "It was," a British officer wrote,

> a glorious and imposing spectacle to behold these noble ships standing up the vast bay of the Chesapeake, into the very heart of America . . . The flags of three British admirals . . . proudly flying at their respective vessels.

On August 19, 1814, British land and sea forces landed at Benedict, Maryland, and five days later routed the American forces at Bladensburg, Maryland, then entered the nation's capital and burned it. While the nation looked toward the Potomac, the British returned to their ships and ultimately set forth to chastise Baltimore, the nation's third largest city. Within three weeks the tide of the war on the Chesapeake would be changed at the headwaters of the Patapsco River.

A series of events began to unfold that would eventually inspire a young lawyer-poet to express his patriotism so eloquently that he would write a poem that became our National Anthem. The history of the Battle of Baltimore is best written by those who participated in that conflict. Their narrative accounts, which so often have intrigued historians, are the strakes of this small volume, with the occasional remarks of the author to fill in the seams.

I hope this small volume will contribute to Baltimore's maritime heritage, and a further appreciation of the gallant defense made by these marine companies who hastened to the call of duty in September of 1814.

1 ☆

FORT MCHENRY AND
THE NATIONAL DEFENSE,
1783–1813

The winds and seas are Britain's wide domain, and not a sail but by permission spreads!
> —*from the masthead of the* Niles' Weekly Register

In the years following the signing of the Treaty of Paris, which ended the American Revolution in 1783, and the adoption of the Federal Constitution in 1787, the young United States of America looked forward to economic recovery and a period of peaceful existence. However, across the Atlantic, relations between England and France had continued to deteriorate until, in 1793, England declared a war on France that lasted for the next two decades. Alarmed for the safety of American coastal ports and trade, in 1794 Congress passed legislation to form a national navy (under the War Department) with a nucleus of six frigates.[1]

That same year Congress approved additional legislation for the building of fortifications along the coast. In Maryland, leaders of the General Assembly offered the federal government the following resolution:

> Whereas, the United States may think it necessary to erect a fort, arsenal, or other military works or building on Whetstone Point for public defense; therefore, Resolved, that upon application of the President of the United States to the Governor for permission to erect a fort, arsenal, or other military works on the said Point for the purpose aforesaid, the Governor shall and may grant the same.[2]

The proposed site of the fort was located on a narrow peninsula of land known as Whetstone Point, at the confluence of the North West and Ferry branches of the Patapsco River. As a strategic location, it commanded the entrance to the shipbuilding and arsenal facilities of Fell's Point. A French-educated military engineer, John Jacob Ulrich Rivardi, was appointed by Secretary of War Henry Knox to plan a fortification to defend Baltimore harbor; however, due to economic limitations, Rivardi was only able to build and improve upon an existing earthen star fort (Fort Whetstone) erected in 1776.

Under the supervision of Lieutenant Samuel Dodge, the redoubt had been upgraded by the summer of 1797 and consisted primarily of two water batteries, a wooden barracks, and two small bastions with no brickwork employed. Despite minor improvements, the redoubt lacked any substantial defense against a well-calculated naval attack.[3]

By 1798, during the administration of President John Adams, relations with France had deteriorated and Congress appropriated funds for coastal defense works and the formation of a Department of the Navy.[4] The primary proponent of the coastal defense legislation was Secretary of War James McHenry, an adopted Marylander.

Born in Ballymena County, Antrim, Ireland, in 1753, McHenry emigrated to Philadelphia shortly before the American Revolution and studied medicine. During the war, he served as a surgeon and as secretary to General George Washington. After the war he became active as a Federalist in Maryland politics, representing the state at the Constitutional Convention, and later was appointed secretary of war, serving under Adams from 1796 to 1800.[5]

McHenry appointed French engineer Major Louis Tousard, a respected military strategist, to submit "a plan and estimate if such additions heretofore may be considered absolutely indispensable for the protection of the city." Tousard, rather than risk his professional reputation, since funds were insufficient, handed his plans over to a citizens' committee which agreed to raise additional funds and supervise the construction.[6]

In the autumn of 1799, with Tousard's plan in hand and the necessary funds, McHenry appointed a third French engineer to complete the fort.

I have employed on the fortifications erecting at Baltimore in the capacity of Enginneer, a French Gentleman of the name Foncin, and that evidence of ability in his profession by correcting errors of much consequence, in the original plan of the works, as well as of assiduity in Superintending and directing their progress, in-

duced me to raise the compensation he was first engaged at. This
Gentleman I would recommend to be continued in employ as
heretofore.[7]

By 1802, the masonry Star Fort was essentially finished and
manned by an incomplete company of artillery under the command
of Captain Staats Morris.[8] In honor of the man responsible for its
existence, the fort was named Fort McHenry. In the ensuing years,
Fort McHenry received minor maintenance and improvements that
were performed by the garrison. In 1811, the secretary of war summarized the completed works:

> . . . Fort McHenry . . . is a regular pentagon of masonry, cal-
> culated for thirty guns, a water battery, with ten heavy guns
> mounted, a brick magazine that will contain three hundred bar-
> rels of powder, with [four] brick barracks for two companies of
> men and officers; without the fort, a wooden barrack for one
> company, also a brick store and gun house.[9]

While the United States maintained a peaceful military establishment and struggled to keep her maritime neutrality, the war between
England and France threatened to spread across the Atlantic. To
maintain her naval superiority, Britain had a constant need for crews,
which led her to a policy of boarding American vessels and im-
pressing seamen into service aboard English vessels. This policy of
impressment extended to naturalized American seamen as well.

By 1812, the United States found herself drifting toward a war she
was militarily unprepared to wage. During the presidency of Thomas
Jefferson (1801-1809), the desire for "economy" resulted in the re-
duction of internal taxes and military expenditures. The reservoir of
state militia troops constituted the nation's primary defense force in
lieu of maintaining a large and costly regular army.

In 1812, under the new administration of President James Madison, Congress was controlled by the "War Hawks," those members
who favored settlement expansion, both in the northwest to gain
control of the British fur trade, and in the south to acquire Florida.
On June 18, 1812, the United States formally declared war on Great
Britain. In the final passage of the *Act*, the vote was nineteen to
thirteen in the Senate and, in the House, seventy-nine to forty-nine.

Fortunately for the United States, England was preoccupied with the
war in Europe, with her army and navy primarily committed to Lord

Wellington's Iberian Peninsula Campaign against Napoleon. This prevented her from sending any large expeditionary force to America. With a British force available on the Canadian frontier protecting her interest, she concentrated her efforts there, and consequently confined her opening campaign against America to that region.

In the summer of 1812, contingents of the regular army and detachments of the Maryland Militia marched northward from Baltimore under the command of Colonel William H. Winder. Earlier in the year, Congress had passed an *Act* "to raise an additional military force" for the enlistment of federal troops to serve for five years, or the duration of the war.[10]

The response to the call of arms in Baltimore was met with "astonishing success and activity," the *Niles' Weekly Register* reported, and "promises to proceed vigorously."[11] Citizen-entrepreneurs acted swiftly to the declaration of war by obtaining official U. S. government commissions called "letters of marque and reprisal," which authorized private citizens to outfit vessels, usually brigs or schooners, known as privateers, to capture the "goods and effects" of Britain's merchant fleet.

In the years prior to the war, Baltimore shipbuilders became well known for their craftsmanship in developing swift clippers whose chief characteristic was long raking masts capable of supporting an enormous amount of canvas. Historian Henry Adams described a typical privateer as being

> armed with one long pivot-gun, and 6 to 8 lighter guns in broadside; carrying crews which varied from one hundred and twenty to one hundred and sixty men; swift enough to escape under most circumstances even a frigate, and strong enough to capture any armed merchantman.[12]

For privateer owners to receive a profitable return on their investment and pay the ship's crew, the seized merchant vessel, manned by a small "prize crew" from the privateer, was taken to a safe port. However, the captured vessel then ran the risk of being recaptured by the British navy and her crew sent to prison. If successful in reaching port, the privateer was later substantially rewarded. Here the "prize vessel," after a prize court examined the legality of her capture, her stores, armament, and the vessel itself, was sold at public auction, and the profits then distributed among her owners and crew. [13]

Within a month after the declaration of war, nearly a dozen privateers had cleared the port of Baltimore. Hezekiah Niles in his weekly newspaper stated that:

> . . . by licensing private armed vessels the whole naval force of the nation is truly brought to bear on the foe; and while the contest lasts, that it may have the speedier termination, let every individual contribute his mite, in the best way he can, to distress and harass the enemy; and compel him to peace. [14]

In the months that followed, Baltimore naval yards, ship chandlers, iron foundries, etc., experienced a flurry of economic activity caused by those citizen-entrepreneurs who invested wisely with prudence and patriotism. Because of the astonishing success that privately armed vessels had against Britain's merchant fleet in the first months of the war, the British government was prompted to take a due course of reprisal. With mounting pressure from her merchant interests at home, England officially declared war on America on October 12, 1812. Later, by proclamation on December 12, 1812, England claimed the Delaware and Chesapeake bays to be in a state of rigid naval blockade. As Baltimore continued to build, outfit, and send her private navy to sea, a British squadron of warships set forth from England to seal the tidewater outlet of the Chesapeake Bay.

2 ☆ ☆

FORT MCHENRY: SPRING 1813

On the morning of February 4, 1813, a British squadron entered the Virginia Capes and dropped anchor in Hampton Roads, Virginia, effecting a naval blockade at the mouth of the Chesapeake Bay. On board HMS *Marlborough*, 74 guns, Rear Admiral Sir George Cockburn (pronounced Cō-burn) surveyed his command which included frigates, ships of the line, sloops, and numerous shallow-draft landing launches.

Cockburn, at forty-two years of age, an impetuous and resourceful naval veteran, began his invasion of the Chesapeake Bay's tidewater towns and tobacco ports. Cockburn's strategy for the Chesapeake campaign was explained later by William Milbourne James in *The Naval History of Great Britain*.

> The rear-admiral's system . . . was to land without offering molestation to the unopposing inhabitants, either in their persons or properties; to capture or destroy all articles of merchandize and munitions of war; to be allowed to take off, upon paying the full market price, all such cattle and supplies as the British squadron might require, but, should resistance be offered, or menaces held out, to consider the town a fortified post, and the male inhabitants as soldiers; the one to be destroyed, the other, with their cattle and stock, to be captured . . .[1]

In March, Cockburn's force of ten warships was reinforced by a naval squadron under the command of Admiral Sir John Borlase

Warren, commander in chief of the North American Station. Although Cockburn's superior, the elderly Admiral Warren ventured to leave the rigorous duties of warfare to the young and energetic rear admiral. The British land forces that accompanied the two squadrons were at best defensive detachments, too small for an extensive campaign on land, but effective enough for a display of force in a war of attrition. The presence of the British navy in the bay prompted local tidewater communities to reestablish their independent militia companies, and the larger cities of Norfolk, Annapolis, and Baltimore to reinforce their coastal defenses.

In Baltimore, Major General Samuel Smith, commander of the Third Division of the Maryland Volunteer Militia, began to organize the city's defense. As the months wore on, the citizens of Baltimore discovered that Smith was the ideal man for the task. He was a respected veteran officer of the Revolutionary War, elected to the House of Representatives in 1783 and to the U. S. Senate in 1803.

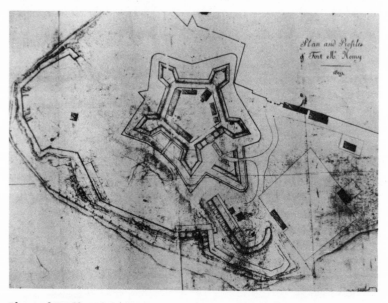

Plan and Profiles of Fort McHenry and Marine Batteries, 1819. Courtesy of the National Park Service.

Smith's political influence provided him with federal and local support for Baltimore's military activities.

On March 12, 1813, Smith wrote Maryland Governor Levin Winder,

> The vicinity of the enemy and facility with which he might pass a force suddenly against the city makes it necessary to be in a state of preparation to repel any attempt that may be made.[2]

Following a personal inspection of Baltimore's defenses, particularly Fort McHenry, the governor authorized Smith "to take the earliest opportunity of making the necessary arrangements of the militia for the defense of the Port of Baltimore."[3] The most pressing concern was Fort McHenry.

In a letter to Secretary of War John Armstrong, Smith listed the fort's deficiencies by stating, "the fort was not in a condition to repel a serious attack from a formidable British fleet."[4] On March 27, Colonel Joseph G. Swift of the U. S. Corps of Engineers inspected the fort and submitted to Major Lloyd Beall, First Regiment of Artillerists, and commander of the fort, a report of work to be done. Major Beall had been in command of Fort Washington on the Potomac River when ordered by the War Department to relieve Captain George Armistead at Fort McHenry on April 9, 1812.[5]

Some of the improvements Colonel Swift suggested were to platform the lower gun batteries, construct three hot shot furnaces, dig a five-foot counterscarp around the fort, and fill in the earthen embrasures within the bastions of the fort to allow the cannon to be fired *en-barbette*.[6] Under the supervision of engineers, civilian work details, many of whom consisted of free black tradesmen, were employed to prepare the works.

Skilled mechanics from the shipyards of Fell's Point were obtained to construct naval gun carriages and mount cannons acquired from the city's naval stores. Major Lloyd Beall informed the secretary of war that the French consul in Baltimore had loaned him the naval guns from the French Man-of-War *L'Eole*. In 1806, the *L'Eole*, after a severe storm off the Virginia Capes, had been towed to Baltimore, and in 1808, was broken up and sold at auction, minus her armament. Her guns consisted of twenty-eight 36-pounders and twenty-eight 18-pounders, a total of fifty-six naval cannon.[7]

On April 16, as Baltimore was still preparing her defenses, a British squadron made its appearance at the mouth of the Patapsco River, sending the city into a state of alarm. The city's militia forces and Fort McHenry's garrison of fifty-two regulars provided a show of Baltimore's readiness to defend herself. The squadron, having presumably taken depth soundings of the river approaches, finally withdrew a week later.

During the British stay, a schooner under a flag of truce, with the pretext of sending dispatches, had an ample opportunity to examine the fort's batteries. They were informed by an American vessel that the French guns of the heaviest caliber had been mounted.[8]

The April appearance of the British enabled the city to secure limited federal and local assistance to increase the harbor defenses. The city council created a Committee of Public Supply to obtain loans from banks and citizens to purchase arms and equipment, with the idea that they would later be reimbursed by the federal government.[9]

While Smith continued to provide the necessary measures to defend Baltimore, a controversy over his legal right to command became an issue to be immediately resolved. Smith's sole claim of command rested upon the governor's vague order of March 13. When the British threatened the city, the secretary of war had ordered Governor Winder to bring into federal service the Maryland Volunteer Militia, part of which was Smith's own Third Brigade. To command these, Winder nominated Brigadier General Henry Miller of Baltimore, a friend of the secretary of war. Consequently, Secretary of War Armstrong immediately issued him a commission in the regular army. Thus for the moment, Miller, superseding Major Beall, commanded Fort McHenry's garrison and those militia troops brought into federal service.[10]

Smith, uncertain of who had command of the fort, wrote to Armstrong on May 6:

> Gen'l Miller assumed an independent command yesterday without any men except the 52 regulars & no person knows whom to obey. For myself, I wish to know distinctly, who has command of this station, whether there is to be one General in Chief or two Generals each having a separate & distinct command.[11]

No sooner had Smith finished writing to the secretary when he was informed that Colonel Abrams Y. Nicoll, newly appointed inspector general of the army, had arrived to command the fort.[12] The confusion as to who was in command of the fort's regulars and the city's militia forces was of great concern especially to Smith. The next day Smith sent his aide-de-camp, Isaac McKim, to Annapolis to confer with the governor as to who had command of Baltimore. On May 19, the governor responded:

> The meaning of the order [of March 13] was that you would proceed to complete the organization of the militia under your command and place them in the best possible state of defense, of course your commission as Major General commenced from that period.[13]

Thus, the governor had clearly established Smith as commander in chief of Baltimore's militia troops. The defensive measures regarding Fort McHenry and Major Beall became an increasing problem to Smith. His legal authority covered only the command of the militia forces.

Although Beall allowed two companies of militia artillery and a regiment of infantry in turn to drill weekly at the fort, no provision was made for them to be regularly stationed there.[14] The fort was under the authority of the War Department. Colonel Nicoll was still in command when Smith impressed upon him the yet unresolved problems concerning Major Beall on May 8:

—The removal of women from the fort
—The use of available quarters within the fort to house militia artillerist and infantry
—The assigning of quarters for militia officers
—And the assigning of quarters outside the fort for the Corps of Seamen [a naval militia artillery company].[15]

Meanwhile, Colonel Nicoll had addressed the War Department on May 9 requesting artillery manuals.

> Colonel [David] Harris who commands a regiment of Baltimore Artillery (two companies of which are at this post) appears very detious [desirous] as well as his officers of acquiring a knowledge of their duties as Artillerists. I therefore consider it a favor if you will forward one by mail a copy of the "Exercise for Garrison and Field Ordnance" for those gentlemen . . .[16]

On May 19, Colonel Nicoll wrote to Major Charles K. Gardner, the Assistant-Adjutant General of the War Department, and expressed support for Major Beall at Fort McHenry.

> . . . In justice to Major Beall I think it my duty to state that his company [First Regiment of Artillerists] in appearance, subordination, and discipline is equal to any in the regiment, and that his utmost exertions have been used to place this work in the most complete state of affairs . . .[17]

In late May, General Smith returned to Washington to resume his seat in the U. S. Senate. This gave him the opportunity to confer personally with Secretary Armstrong and other officials regarding Baltimore's defenses. While Smith was in Washington, he had not been forgotten by his constituents. In the eyes of Baltimore's leading citizens and the Committee of Public Supply, he was the only man qualified to direct the defense of their city. In July, a delegation traveled to the War Department to support Smith's proposal to replace Major Beall with a more capable commander.

However, the delegation could not obtain any satisfactory response upon their request for arms, an increase of federal troops, and additional funds from the federal government, unless an attack was imminent. "In the meantime," the delegation reported,

> great reliance was placed on our numbers, energies and resources, which it was approved, with the aid of Major Armistead's command, would be adequate to a successful resistance of the enemy, until reinforcements could be added.[18]

Despite Colonel Nicoll's complimentary report of Beall's conduct, Secretary Armstrong had already directed the fort's former commander, Major George Armistead "to take command of Fort McHenry & its dependencies during the indisposition of Major Beall, until further orders."[19] This official action by the Secretary exceedingly pleased Smith and also relieved him of any further doubts regarding the fort's defensive command.

Major Armistead was quite familiar with Fort McHenry, having been second in command from 1809 to 1812. His prior position was Assistant Military Agent at Fort Niagara, New York, from 1802 to 1807. In 1812, he was reassigned to Fort Niagara and on March 3, 1813, he received a commission as Major in the Third Regiment of Artillery. He subsequently distinguished himself at the capture of Fort George, Upper Canada, and was given the honor of carrying the captured British flags to Washington.[20]

Having assumed command, Armistead lost no time in responding to Smith's requests. On July 13, he wrote to Smith (who had returned to Baltimore) on the subject of the harbor defenses.

> Sir, Agreeable to your request it will require to place this post in a complete state of defense nine 24-pounders or Eighteens; for the Patapsco Battery, ten 24-pounders. I would also recommend two 10-inch mortars for this post and at least 25 spherical shot for each gun. A Six-Gun Battery on the Lazaretto Point, a sod work, would add considerably to the defense and safety of Baltimore . . .[21]

The Patapsco Battery to which Armistead referred was already under construction. The city had requested from the War Department an additional rear defense work for Fort McHenry on the Ferry Branch. Known as the Spring Garden Battery during its initial stages of construction, it was designed by Colonel Decius Wadsworth, Chief Ordnance Officer of the War Department, at the city's expense.[22]

By December 1813, Captain Samuel Babcock, U. S. Corps of Engineers, reported that the new battery was capable of receiving ten or twelve guns for a battery *en-barbette*, with quarters for a company of men, a guard house, and a powder magazine.[23] In the spring of 1814, the new battery was named Fort Covington, after Brigadier General Leonard Covington, a Marylander who had been killed in Upper Canada a few months before.[24] Two other shore gun batteries, Battery Babcock and the Lazaretto Battery, were also under construction.

On July 27, 1813, Armistead was authorized by the Secretary of War to receive Captain Joseph Hopper Nicholson's newly organized militia artillery company of Baltimore Fencibles "in the event of the enemy's approach" as part of his defense.[25] The arrival of Captain Nicholson's company of U. S. volunteers prompted a cordial relationship between the two commanders and an answer to the fort's need of additional reinforcements.

Nicholson's company represented the elite of Baltimore's mercantile society—"wealthy merchants and bankers who had invested in the city's profitable privateers, each standing to lose a great deal should the British capture Baltimore."[26] Nicholson's position, however, was not easily obtained. As chief judge of the sixth judicial district and court of appeals of Maryland, state law prevented him from obtaining a commission in the militia. Eager to serve, he applied to the secretary of war to direct Major Armistead to receive his company, which Armstrong readily granted.[27]

Although under the exclusive authority of the United States, the Baltimore Fencibles were nominally attached to Colonel David Harris's First Regiment of Artillery for all purposes of parade and exercise.[28]

With the questions of Fort McHenry's command and Smith's extent of authority over the city's militia forces finally resolved, the only remaining variable was the uncertainty of when the British would attack.

3 ☆ ☆ ☆

FELL'S POINT RENDEZVOUS

These Lads of the Ocean A-Shore . . .
—Niles' Weekly Register, *June 5, 1813*

THE FIRST MARINE ARTILLERY OF THE UNION

With Rear Admiral George Cockburn's British naval squadron in the bay threatening to attack Baltimore, General Smith needed experienced gun crews to man the gun batteries and city barges that were under construction. The blockade of the bay had prompted many seamen to seek other seaports as a means of securing a profitable livelihood, especially when serving upon American privateers.[1]

Places for recruitment in various naval and militia services were found throughout the city, but nowhere more abundantly than in Fell's Point, a flourishing maritime community of merchants, sea captains, and naval mechanics, many of whom were actively employed in the privateer trade. The shipyards of Joseph Despeaux, William Price, Thomas Kemp, and William Parsons were kept busy building the barges and privateers that were to be outfitted with the armaments of war. Boarding houses and taverns on the Point had served adequately for recruiting services since 1797 when the first crew of the United States Frigate *Constellation* had been enlisted.

In the spring of 1813, the Committee of Public Supply opened a rendezvous for seamen and landsmen to man the marine batteries at Fort McHenry. A public notice appeared in the daily paper, the *Baltimore American & Commercial Daily Advertizer*, on March 20:

> The First Marine Artillery of the Union; having met agreeable to public service, Resolved to invite all Masters and Mates of Vessels

belonging to or in this port, who have the interest of their Country and Seamen's Rights at heart, to meet at Pamphilion's Hotel, on MONDAY EVENING, the 22nd inst., at 6 o'clock, for the purpose of joining them in filling the ranks and choosing officers. It is sanguinely expected and wished that all of the above descriptions of citizens will flock to this laudable undertaking.[2]

By May, General Smith was able to report to the committee that he had, according to their instructions, organized a Corps of Seamen (by which name they were commonly referred) and placed them under the command of Captain George Stiles.

Stiles, a former sea captain during the quasi-war with France, had originally organized the corps in 1808. Their daily presence on Stiles's wharf evoked "a peculiar tribute of respect" from the local citizenry for their "unabated vigour and unflagging spirit."[3] The corps' strength now mustered nearly two hundred officers and enlisted men.

The corps was divided into two companies of seventy-five men each, to be commanded by Captain Solomon Rutter and Captain Matthew Simmones Bunbury. In a letter addressed to the Committee on May 15, Smith reported:

> The whole are bound by written articles signed by each, to do duty either in boats or fortifications for three months from the day of signing, unless sooner discharged, to conform and obey the command of their officers in the same manner as if they were in actual service at sea, for which they are to receive Sixteen Dollars per month. This highly important corps have been employed in the Barges, in fixing the booms, transporting and mounting of cannons, placing the hulks, making wads for the guns, and in training to the exercise of the cannon . . .[4]

The city's enlistment of seamen for harbor defense at $16 per month had a certain advantage over the U. S. Navy pay of $10 to $12 per month being offered by Captain Charles Gordon, Commandant of the Baltimore Naval Station. In a letter to Smith on April 30, Gordon expressed sincere concern over the Committee's "impropriety of one rendezvous offering more than the other . . . I was about to offer a bounty of $10 as an inducement . . . but on hearing of the $16 rendezvous I revoked the order, fearful it might induce the opposite rendezvous to bid above us . . ."[5]

Gordon, whose command comprised about one hundred seamen, had been ordered to Baltimore shortly before the war. Prior to the British blockade, nine of his ten gunboats had been ordered to the Norfolk Station. Gunboat *No. 138*, left in Baltimore, was equipped with one long 24-pounder and two 12-pound carronades.[6] Smith, on Gordon's behalf, wrote Secretary of the Navy William Jones on March 13 for the return of the gunboats. In response, Smith was informed that the gunboats could not be withdrawn then, but that Gordon should continue to cooperate with the city.[7]

To increase Gordon's Baltimore flotilla, the secretary gave permission in May for Gordon to lease four privateer schooners at Baltimore.[8] Smith volunteered to lend the services of the First Marine Artillery and the city barges in a cooperative venture of posting guard below the fort. This agreement proved beneficial to both parties and was continued successfully through the summer of 1813.

The daily presence of the city barges on the Patapsco River added to the security of a large iron works foundry owned by John Dorsey on Curtis Creek, five miles below Fort McHenry. Under contract by the navy and army for one hundred carronades and cannon shot, Decius Wadsworth, Chief Ordnance Officer for the War Department, was prompted to consider "the preservation of the establishment . . . in part a national object." To protect it further, a detachment of the Maryland Volunteer Militia Infantry was stationed on the site, upon orders from Governor Winder.[9]

One of the most effective defense measures taken by Smith was the placement of a chain-mast boom across the North West Branch. On May 4, Captain Rutter was ordered with his command

> . . . to lay booms of old or new masts connected by strong iron chains, and bolts riveted through the ends of each mast from the shore of Gorsuch [Lazaretto] Point to the shore on Whetstone Point, supported by anchors or poles at each end, and [to extend] in front of the Marine Battery, at a distance of 150 yards from the shore, to extend to the steep bank [on the Ferry Branch] . . .[10]

To impede any further unwarranted entry into the channel, Captain Rutter was entrusted with maintaining several merchant vessels near the Lazaretto. Here they could easily be sunk to block the channel behind the booms.

The city also contracted the building of nine barges which were completed in a relatively short time. In a letter to the Committee of Public Supply on May 18, Smith requested that each boat should be

> . . . from 65 to 70 feet long, prepared for oars, to mount a 32-pounder in the bow and stern and constructed to sail equally well with either end for a bow . . . the whole ought to be built by contract and the first in the water in three weeks . . .[11]

Each barge was numbered and assigned an American flag and a numeral flag to fly below it. Thomas Galloway, a professional painter, was paid $2.50 to paint the numeral flags. It would be these barges that later defended the channel in September 1814.[12]

As the outfitting of the barges continued, Captain Stiles's corps was busily involved in two other important enterprises. First, the corps assisted in the construction of the upper and lower gun batteries for the French naval guns. By May 1813, nearly thirty-six guns had been mounted on naval carriages at Fort McHenry. To honor the seamen's labor in completing it, the fortification received the name Marine Battery.[13] Second, another battery was erected one and one-half miles west of the fort on the Ferry Branch. Known as Battery Babcock, after Captain Samuel Babcock who supervised the city-financed work, it mounted six French 18-pounders behind an earthen breastwork four feet high with a magazine in the rear. Because of its simple design, the fortification was completed in a short time, and often was referred to as the "Sailor's Battery," after the men who built and garrisoned it.[14]

Through the summer of 1813, the First Marine Artillery and Captain Gordon's Baltimore Flotilla maintained a constant watch on the Patapsco River near North Point. This afforded them a view down the bay to Annapolis for approaching enemy vessels. The relationship of command between Captain Stiles and Captain Gordon was again clarified by General Smith on August 9:

> Ordered, that Captain Stiles lend to Captain Gordon of the U. S. Navy use of the City Barges to be manned and armed from the flotilla under his command. That he cooperate with Captain Gordon with the City Barges for the defense of the river and

security of Fort McHenry and the City [Babcock] Battery by rowing guard or in any other way which he may deem necessary & proper on consultation with Capt. Gordon . . .[15]

Smith issued these orders because on August 8, the British had established a temporary naval base on Kent Island on the Eastern Shore. With the consent of Major Armistead, Smith ordered the Marine Artillery "to be quartered within the garrison of Fort McHenry from sunset to sunrise."[16] In addition to Stiles's command, a detachment of the Thirty-Eighth U. S. Infantry under Major Samuel Lane was ordered to the fort.[17]

Smith ordered a system of communication between the city barges at North Point and Fort McHenry to survey the movement of the enemy. Captain Rutter was instructed "to point a Blue Jack as a signal in case the enemy are standing down the bay and a White Jack if the enemy are coming up the bay."[18]

The reconnaissance exercises of the British squadron prompted Smith to increase the readiness of the Corps of Seamen and the militia companies assigned to the fort. On August 23, Captain Rutter was able to report to Smith,

. . . I perceived the Union Jack, which the enemy had hoisted on the top of a house on Kent Island, is down, and a White flag hoisted in place of it.[19]

Although the city's militia forces were called into federal service, the British withdrew from the bay for winter quarters at Bermuda. On August 29, Captain Rutter resigned from the Corps of Seamen, as he had been appointed second in command of the newly organized U. S. Chesapeake Flotilla under Commodore Joshua Barney.[20]

Captain Matthew Bunbury resigned in October to command one of the two U. S. Sea Fencible companies that was to defend Fort McHenry in September 1814.[21] Fatigued by his various duties, Bunbury explained in a letter to the Committee of Public Supply on October 14:

. . . My having to keep constant guard at night, up all day at the Lazaretto, frequently in town on duty, instructions to write to the Commanders of the Galley & Barges, every morning . . . kept me continually employed & very little rest at night . . .[22]

In the spring of 1814, a proposal for a floating battery to be propelled by steam was being considered by Congress. Initially designed by Robert Fulton, the steam battery (named *Demologos*) was conceived as a heavily armed catamaran-type steamboat mounting several large caliber cannon. In an effort to attract the interest and funds of the federal government, a model was constructed and inspected by various naval officers.

On March 9, 1814, Congress, via the Senate Naval Affairs Committee, passed a bill for the construction of "one or more" floating batteries. The prototype to be built in New York would, if approved, be followed by others.[23]

In Baltimore, plans for a similar battery, designed to carry thirty 32-pounders, were submitted by Captain George Stiles at the mayor's office on March 2, 1814. The model was thereafter placed in Stiles's house for public viewing and to raise $150,000 in subscriptions for its construction.[24]

Stiles exhibited his model to the Navy Department on March 16; however, Secretary Jones expressed some doubt as to the engine and paddle designs. In a private letter to Judge Joseph H. Nicholson, Jones addressed his view that the "military expenditure is frightful," and there would be difficulty in acquiring any federal assistance until the prototype was proven sound. Besides, the formation of Joshua Barney's U. S. Chesapeake Flotilla of gunboats could, with the assistance of federal troops, adequately protect the bay.[25] In the months to follow, the citizens of Baltimore began to raise the funds to build Baltimore's steam battery. However, by the end of 1814, and with the war's end in sight, Stiles's steam battery project was discontinued, as he was unable to secure additional federal funds.[26]

The effectiveness of the Corps of Seamen in 1813 led Smith and the Committee of Public Supply to restore them again in 1814. In the summer of 1814, during a recruitment drive, Captain Stiles ordered the following notice to be placed in the papers of Baltimore.[27]

FIRST MARINE ARTILLERY OF THE UNION
Meet at your gun house at 3 o'clock on *Saturday next*, in uniform complete, to exercise the heavy field ordnance. Knowing as you do, that the weight of this metal requires much strength, renders it unnecessary for any entreaties to be advanced by your captain, for your prompt attendance. The object of this early hour is to

admit, agreeable to your constitution, new members, *we have a right* to expect every master and mate in port. The cloud gathers fast and heavy in the East, and all hands are called; few, very few, are the number of masters and mates belonging to this port that will be justified in excusing themselves from service by one of their skippers not being so firm as the other, or that he has seen five and forty; if he cannot sponge and ram as well as his mess-mates, he can pass a cartridge. It is well known by all Tars the *just stigm[a]*, that is fixed by the ship's crew on the man that skulks below, or under the lee of the long boat, when all hands are called; their services were not wanting until the present, but now your city calls all to arms, you are therefore invited and entreated to fall into our ranks.

Many 18-pounders are already manned and many more fit for service; come and join as we give a long pull, a strong pull, and a pull altogether—and *save the ship.*

By order of the Captain.

ROBERT G. HENDERSON, Sec'y

July 20 [1814]

The U. S. Marine Corps

The twenty dollars being offered at the U. S. Marine Corps recruitment rendezvous at No. 2 Fell's Point Market in the spring of 1813 seemed a rich inducement for those landsmen and seamen out of employment. Lieutenant Benjamin Hyde, the recruiting officer in Baltimore, provided an opportunity for those men to man the frigates and sloops of war of the U. S. Navy. On May 13, 1813, he placed a recruitment notice in the *Baltimore Patriot.*

To Men of Courage, Enterprize, and Patriotism
At the present crises, you are called on by every motive of honor to rank yourselfs among the defenders and avengers of your Country. Already have the Naval Heroes of Columbia achieved for themselves immortal glory; and a new opportunity is now offered to enter your names on the roll of fame.

You are invited to rank yourselfs under the Standard of your Country, in a service, which will not merely distinguish, but reward you. A Rendezvous for the Marine Service is now opened at the home of Landlord Peter Tebo, Fell's Point Market No. 2, where such of you as are disposed to earn laurels and gain Prize Money, are invited to enter this promising service.

Twenty Dollars Bounty, and three months advanced pay, will be given, in the outset. Your pay and rations will be liberal; and again you are reminded, that an opportunity is offered for enriching yourselfs with Prize Money. The gallant conquerors on board the *Constitution* have divided 150 Dollars per man. Come then, there is no time to be lost.

> BENJAMIN HYDE
> Lieut. of Marines[28]

At the beginning of the War of 1812, the Marine Corps strength was an estimated one thousand officers and enlisted men, less than half its authorized complement. Recruitment became a continual problem during the war, since prospective recruits could enlist in other services that offered more incentives. On May 16, 1813, Lieutenant Hyde wrote to Marine Commandant Franklin Wharton in Washington:

> Sir, I am sorry to say that I have not been able as yet to recruit a single man; the town [of Baltimore] at this time is so full of rendezvous recruiting for the army, particularly the 36th [U. S. Infantry] Regt. who are giving 40 Dollars Bounty and 8 Dollars per month pay and enlisting only for 12 months. Those who are disposed to enlist consider the above a much greater inducement than I am at liberty to offer. However, I have reason to think that I know of 2 or 3 likely young men that I believe will enlist . . .[29]

Lieutenant Hyde's efforts had been troubled by the recent organization by Congress of the Thirty-Sixth and Thirty-Eighth U. S. Infantry Regiments, designed particularly for the defense of Maryland.[30] The enlistment bounty of $40 was in addition to the recently increased army monthly pay of $8, including a bounty land warrant for 160 acres of land upon discharge.[31]

In May 1813, Lieutenant William Rogers, a recruiting officer of the Thirty-Sixth Regiment, opened his rendezvous on Bond Street, Fell's Point—four doors from the Marine Corps quarters.[32] Recruitment in Baltimore during the war proved inadequate, despite a $20 enlistment bounty authorized by the commandant.[33] Those who enlisted, however, provided service in Baltimore aboard the Baltimore Flotilla in 1813 and guarded the naval shipyards.

In August 1813, Commandant Wharton created a battalion of one hundred twenty marines at Washington, commanded by Corps Adjutant Captain Samuel Miller. He was ordered to cooperate with the U. S. Chesapeake Flotilla, commanded by Commodore Joshua Barney, on the Patuxent River. A year later, this well-trained battalion served with valor on the field at Bladensburg, Maryland, in an ill-fated attempt to defend the nation's capital.[34]

The U. S. Marines stationed in Baltimore by February 1814 consisted of the following detachments:[35]

On board the U. S. Sloop of War *Erie* 20
On board the U. S. Sloop of War *Ontario* 20
Baltimore Navy Yard 11

However, on April 12, the Secretary of the Navy ordered the marine guards of the *Erie* and *Ontario* to be sent to Sackets Harbor on Lake Ontario.[36] By July 1814, the marine station at Baltimore consisted of one sergeant (commanding), two corporals, and nine privates.[37]

On August 4, 1814, with a large British naval force expected to arrive in the Chesapeake, the commandant authorized Captain Alfred Grayson in Annapolis to proceed to Baltimore.

. . . It will be most proper, I conceive, for you to fix the Rendezvous near the quarters of the Marine Guard, on the Point, so as to have the advantage of Sergeant [Morris] Palmer's aid & the corporals their in recruiting, & at the same time be enabled to inspect the conduct of that, most probably relaxed detachment, so long without a Commissioned Officer . . . [the recruits] must be passed, as to soundness, by a physician, & your own opinion must govern as to their fitness for the Corps . . . I hope your exertions will be soon successful enough to supply us with a number of men . . .[38]

The U. S. Navy

In September 1813, the main British squadron withdrew from the Chesapeake for winter quarters in Bermuda, leaving a small detachment of vessels behind. In anticipation of their departure, the owners of the four schooners were busily preparing them for privateer duty. With the exception of the *Wasp*, which possessed poor sailing qualities, the *Comet*, *Revenge*, and *Patapsco* successfully cleared Baltimore for sea.

The commander of the *Comet*, Thomas Boyle, was the foremost privateer captain to leave Baltimore. A contemporary historian described Boyle as "a dashing brave man [who] wisely judged when to attack the enemy, and when to retreat, with honor to himself and to the flag under which he sailed . . ."[39] Within a year, Boyle was in command of another vessel that brought upon him the rewards of a successful naval career. This vessel, known as the *Chasseur*, was launched in Fell's Point on December 12, 1812.[40]

The *Comet* and *Chasseur* were built by Thomas Kemp, a Quaker shipbuilder whose shipyard was bounded by Fountain, Fleet, and Washington streets in Fell's Point. Under contract with the Navy Department in 1813, Kemp built two sloops of war, the *Ontario* and *Erie*, both launched in the fall of that year.[41] Congress had authorized construction of the vessels in February, as well as three 36-gun frigates: the USS *Guerriere* in Philadelphia, the USS *Columbia* in the Washington Navy Yard, and the USS *Java* in Baltimore, built at the shipyard of Flannagain and Parsons.[42]

The *Ontario* was placed under the command of Captain Robert T. Spence, who replaced Gordon as Commandant of the Baltimore Naval Station.[43] The *Erie* was commanded by Captain Charles G. Ridgely, a native Baltimorean.[44] During the fall and winter of 1813, both commanders set about the arduous task of preparing their vessels and recruiting seamen before the British blockade was reinforced in the spring.

Among the officers assigned to the *Ontario* was Sailing Master Leonard Hall, who briefly commanded the privateer *Wasp*. Unsuccessful in clearing the Virginia Capes in late summer, the *Wasp* had returned to Baltimore, and Hall signed aboard the *Ontario* in September 1813.[45]

On November 16, 1813, Captain Spence addressed the secretary of the navy, concerning prospective enlistments for the *Ontario*.

> . . . The number of [privateer] schooners that have sailed, and at present fitting out, the high wages given by them for seamen, seem to forbid all hope of obtaining a crew, as speedily as could be wished; and it is with regret I see the *Ontario* without men, while the *Erie* has upward of sixty . . .[46]

To help the *Ontario's* recruitment, Lieutenant Edward McCall was ordered on November 23 to Alexandria, Virginia, by the secretary. His orders were

> to endeavor to recruit as many seamen, Ordinary Seamen and Boys, for the United States Ship *Ontario* as may be practicable, the wages of the seamen $12, Ordinary Seamen and Boys 6 to 10 Dollars per month . . .

McCall had further instructions to enlist at a bounty of $20 if recruitment proved to be slow.[47]

Among the ordinary seamen who had shipped on board the *Ontario* was Gabriel Roulson. He was described as a black man who wore the usual clothing of seamen of his day, a blue roundabout jacket and trousers, a white cotton shirt, tarpaulin hat, striped gingham vest, and a pair of boots. He was one of many black sailors who had enlisted in the various naval services in Baltimore.[48]

Among the military and naval services, an opportunity for officers to exchange sentiments on the war presented itself the evening of February 2, 1814. The distinguished citizens of Baltimore and Mayor Edward Johnson of Baltimore were hosts to Commodore Oliver Hazard Perry. The young commodore was on his way to Newport, Rhode Island, having recently attended the launching of the U. S. Sloop of War *Argus* in Washington.[49]

With nearly three hundred guests in attendance at the Fountain Inn on Light Street, the proprietor, John Barney, furnished an elegant feast with patriotic naval decorations befitting the Hero of Lake Erie. A large transparent painting depicting the moment when Perry had signaled his squadron for "close action," giving him a victory over the British, adorned the front of the hall. Numerous toasts were given. The highlight of the evening was described by a correspondent of the *Niles' Weekly Register:*

> . . . As the several toasts were announced, the music struck up a patriotic air . . . Suddenly the roll of a drum, as if first heard at a great distance, was heard behind the transparency, and every eye was turned that way. The roll grew louder and louder and, having reached its entire force, down came the British flag from the enemy's ship in the foreground of the picture—then the full

band struck up *Yankee Doodle*, and the British flag was hoisted *under* the American ensign . . .[50]

After several concluding toasts in the commodore's presence, Perry rose from the table and presented his own: "Commerce— may she continue to disperse her favors with a liberal hand, on her favorite port—Baltimore."[51] At the time Perry was visiting the city, a new ship, the USS *Java*, was taking shape in the naval yard of Flannagain and Parsons at Fell's Point. Within the year, the twenty-seven-year-old Perry would command her.

On March 12, 1814, the U. S. Sloop of War *Erie* was ready for sea; however, in light of the renewed British blockade of the bay, the secretary of the navy ordered the commanders of the *Ontario* and *Erie* to lay their vessels up and secure their stores in a safe manner.[52] On April 17, Captain Ridgely, with the officers and crew of the *Erie*, were ordered to Sackets Harbor on Lake Ontario, to counter a renewed British offensive to recapture control of that region.[53]

Left in command of the *Erie*, in Ridgely's absence, was Sailing Master George De La Roche, two officers, and twenty men.[54] The petty officers and crew of the *Ontario* were ordered to be transferred to the U. S. Chesapeake Flotilla under Commodore Barney.[55] Commander Spence remained on board the *Ontario* with Sailing Master Leonard Hall and two or three men to take care of the vessel. A U. S. marine guard under Sergeant Palmer was left to protect the two sloops and *Java* at Fell's Point.[56]

THE U. S. CHESAPEAKE FLOTILLA

On November 23, 1812, the 12-gun privateer schooner *Rossie*, commanded by Joshua Barney, sailed into the Patapsco River, ending one of the most sucessful privateer cruises of the war. The *Rossie* had left Baltimore in July 1812 and within three months, captured eighteen English merchantmen, their total exceeding one and a half million dollars.[57]

Barney, apparently not concerned with profits, was consumed with patriotic fervor to do damage to the enemy's public shipping. Later, in a letter to the owners, Barney wrote,

. . . I am sorry my cruise began so late, or I might have done much more injury to the enemy. I find small vessels will no longer answer my purpose and have declined proceeding on another cruise . . .[58]

A native Baltimorean, Barney served with distinction during the American Revolution as a privateer captain, receiving the respect of his seafaring compatriots. In 1795, he received a commission in the French navy and, several years later, obtained the rank of commodore. In 1801, he returned to Baltimore, and in June 1812, upon receiving the news of war, took command of the *Rossie*.[59]

After his cruise, he retired from public life to his new home at Elkridge in Anne Arundel County, Maryland.[60] When Admiral Cockburn's British squadron arrived in the Chesapeake Bay in the spring of 1813, Barney soon reconsidered his position as a country squire. The Baltimore and Annapolis papers were daily recording the forays of Cockburn's naval forces on the bay. Reading the news of attacks and pillage at St. Michaels, Queenstown, Fredericktown, Frenchtown, Georgetown, and Havre de Grace, Barney was rent with patriotic outrage toward a seemingly unassailable enemy.

On July 4, 1813, Joshua Barney, Esq., submitted a plan entitled the "Defense of the Chesapeake Bay &c.," to Secretary of the Navy William Jones:

. . . The Object of the enemy (well known), is the destruction of the City and Navy Yard at Washington, the City and Navy Yard at Norfolk, and the City of Baltimore . . . I am therefore of [the] opinion that the only defense we have in our power, is a kind of barge or row-galley, so constructed, as to draw a small draft of water, to carry oars, light sails, and one heavy gun. These vessels may be built in a short time (say three weeks), men may be had, the City of Baltimore alone, could furnish officers and men for twenty barges, without difficulty. We have in Baltimore 150 masters and mates of vessels, all of whom have seen and some of them have been out in such kind of vessels . . . Such men can be relied upon, and when no further service would be required from them, would again return into merchant service, by which means the officers of the U. S. Navy would not be called into service. Let as many of these barges be built as can be manned, form them into a flying squadron, let them be continually watching and annoying the enemy in our waters, where we have the advantage of shoal water and flats in abundance throughout the Chesapeake Bay . . .[61]

Barney's reference to the "150 masters and mates of vessels" he proposed to use in Baltimore evidently referred to the Marine Artillery under Captain George Stiles. The city of Baltimore had already begun construction of several barges and row galleys for the protection of the port to be manned by Captain Stiles's Corps of Seamen.

While in Newport, Rhode Island, attending to details relating to one of the prizes taken earlier by the *Rossie*, Barney received the secretary's response to his proposal in a letter dated August 20:

> The President of the United States reposing special trust and confidence in your patriotism, valor, fidelity, and abilities has directed this special letter appointing you an Acting Master Commandant in the Navy of the United States for the special purpose of the distinct and separate command (subject only to the direct orders of the Secretary of the Navy) of the United States Flotilla in the upper part of the Chesapeake to consist of such vessels as shall be designated by the Department of the Navy . . .[62]

Barney graciously accepted the appointment and lost no time in returning to Baltimore where the new flotilla was taking shape. In an effort to launch the flotilla, while additional barges were being contracted, the Navy Department purchased the city's row galley *Vigilant* and the barges *No. 5* and *No. 6* on September 29, 1813.[63] The flotilla was reinforced the following February by several barges, and, from the (Norfolk) Potomac Flotilla, the topsail sloop USS *Scorpion*, the row galley *Blacksnake*, the 3-gun schooner *Asp*, and gunboats *No. 137* and *No. 138*.[64]

The secretary authorized Barney to

> . . . open a rendezvous and recruit as many men as will man the whole of the new and old barges . . . being the same pay, and . . . entitled to the same rations, and privileges, as in the Navy of the United States. To be regularly shipped, under articles for 12 months, subject to the rules and regulations for the government of the Navy; but not liable to be drafted into any other service, than that of the Chesapeake Flotilla . . .[65]

Top left: Commodore Joshua Barney, 1818, by Rembrandt Peale. Courtesy of The Peale Museum, Baltimore, Maryland. *Top right:* Lieutenant Colonel George Armistead, 1816, by Rembrandt Peale. Courtesy of The Peale Museum. *Below:* Commodore John Rodgers, 1818-1819, by Charles Willson Peale. Courtesy of the Independence National Historical Park Collection, National Park Service.

Barney began his recruitment in late 1813, placing weekly notices in the various Baltimore papers.

CHESAPEAKE FLOTILLA
Where an honorable and comfortable situation offers to men out of employ, during the Embargo; where Seamen and Landsmen, will receive two months pay advanced, and half-pay monthly, and single men can provide for aged parents, and widows for helpless children, in the same manner; with the advantage of always being near their families, and not to be drafted into the militia, or turned over into any other service. Apply to the recruiting officer, or JOSHUA BARNEY.
    Com'dt of U. S. Flotilla[66]

Barney's appointment by the secretary prompted Lemuel Taylor, a prominent Baltimore merchant, to discredit Barney in a letter to the Secretary of the Navy on August 20, 1813:

. . . I presume you are acquainted with his Character, but if you are not, permit me to inform you that he is a most abandoned rascal both as to politics and morals and that he is despised by 9/10 of all that have taken an active part in the defense of Balto. and none more than by Capt. George Stiles whose Zeal and activity you must have heard of . . .[67]

This abusive attack on his character outraged Barney. He immediately challenged Taylor to a duel with pistols. Taylor was subsequently wounded, but recovered sufficiently to take part in the defense of Baltimore in 1814.[68]

In turn, Captain Stiles resented Barney because the latter was issued one of two *first* letters of marque and reprisal in June 1812. Stiles, who had been promised the first letter for authorization of his privateer *Nonsuch*, learned of Barney's political maneuvering to acquire the honor for his own command of the *Rossie*. Custom Collector James McCulloch of Baltimore informed officials in Washington that Stiles's commission would remain valid and that a special commission would be, on order of the president, issued to Barney.[69]

This political rivalry and Barney's proposal to recruit the Corps of Seamen as part of his own flotilla produced a pronounced competitiveness between the two commanders as they sought recruits. In February 1814, with recruitment for the flotilla underway, the secretary of the navy attempted to alleviate the situation in the following manner:

> Bay and River-craft men, seamen, ordinary seamen who have families, riggers, and naval mechanics out of employ, will engage in this service under a local commander of capacity and influence, when they will not engage for the regular naval service.[70]

On April 16, 1814, Congress passed an *Act* for the appointment of officers for the flotilla service, thus clarifying the relationship of rank between officers in it and in the regular navy.[71] Barney soon received commissions for two enterprising officers to help command. One of these was Captain Solomon Frazier, whom Barney described as "rich and at ease," a state senator from the Eastern Shore, who intended to quit the senate if the appointment was made.[72] Frazier was appointed a second lieutenant and was ordered to supervise the construction of four barges at St. Michaels, on the Eastern Shore of Maryland, and to recruit men for the service.[73]

In Baltimore, Captain Solomon Rutter, formerly of the Marine Artillery, was appointed first lieutenant and placed second in command under Barney. Barney's decision to obtain their services seemed a sure and effective means of attracting seamen and landsmen who had served under them.

Fifty-year-old Joshua Barney, now commanding the U. S. Chesapeake Flotilla, was well prepared to assume the role of command. On May 24, 1814, the flotilla, consisting of the block-sloop *Scorpion*, gunboats *No. 137* and *No. 138*, the row galley *Vigilant*, the schooner *Asp*, and thirteen barges, left Baltimore and sailed down the Chesapeake Bay.

In the three months to follow, Barney, with his five hundred flotillamen, maneuvered an ever escalating naval duel with the British on the Patuxent River. Gaining valuable time for Baltimore, "this formidable and so much vaunted flotilla" amply secured the naval resources of Rear Admiral Cockburn's attention. Barney's command soon found itself guarding the watery back door to the nation's capital.

THE U. S. SEA FENCIBLES

On the afternoon of January 4, 1814, the following recruitment notice appeared in the daily *Baltimore Patriot & Evening Advertizer*.

SEA FENCIBLES

A number of men are wanted to make up a company of Sea Fencibles. Seamen, or men that are used to rowing and are useful in boats, will be preferred. It will be a comfortable situation for those who are out of employ. The pay is 12 dollars per month, and navy rations; to serve twelve months. No advance, but paid their whole wages monthly. During the winter, unless something unforeseen happens, those that have families can draw their rations, and take them to their homes. They are not liable to be drafted or transferred, and are to act by land or water, as the occasion may require—under their own officers. Those who wish to enter will apply at the rendezvous in Bond Street, No. 59 Market Street, Fell's Point. None need apply but healthy men.

M. SIMMONES BUNBURY

Capt. Sea Fencibles[74]

The establishment of the Sea Fencibles was in imitation of the maritime divisions of the *garde-côte* (coast guard) in France. The primary duty of the unit was to keep a vigilant lookout in the harbors by manning gunboats and coastal fortifications.[75]

In June of 1813, with the British naval blockade in effect, the subject of an increased seaboard defense was submitted to the War Department. The report was addressed to the Honorable Mr. Joseph Anderson, Chairman of the Senate Naval Committee, from Secretary of War John Armstrong.

It stated that

. . . Our Atlantic towns and cities [can] furnish, respectfully, a large number of seafaring men, who, from their hardihood, and habits of life, might be very usefully employed in the defense of the seaboard, particularly in the management of the great guns, whether in fixed or in floating batteries, or in those of position. A corps of great efficiency might be formed out of these men, and on terms much more economical than those necessary to obtain soldiers of the line . . . They may be had at the rate of twelve dollars per month (if subsisted) and without expense on account of clothing . . .[76]

On July 26, 1813, Congress passed "An Act to authorize the raising of a corps of sea fencibles." It authorized the president of the United States

. . . to raise for such term as he may think proper, not exceeding one year, as many companies of sea fencibles as he may deem necessary, not exceeding ten, who may be employed as well on land as on water, for the defense of the ports and harbors of the United States . . .[77]

In 1814, two companies of U. S. Sea Fencibles were stationed at Fort McHenry, under the respective commands of Captain Matthew Bunbury and Captain William H. Addison. Both companies were comprised of men who had served aboard privateers, though many were also skilled in land trades.

Prior to federal service, Captain Bunbury had been employed by the city of Baltimore in the Corps of Seamen, and been charged with the command of Battery Babcock. On October 4, 1813, Bunbury accepted a presidential appointment as a captain of the U. S. Sea Fencibles.[78] On February 10, 1814, the War Department addressed a letter to the commander of Fort McHenry, Major George Armistead.

Sir, Captain Bunbury of the Sea Fencibles is this day instructed to report to you. You will put him, and his recruits on duty at Fort McHenry, or Battery Babcock, as you may judge most proper, and his men must be instructed in the artillery exercise.[79]

Captain Addison's company had been formed with members of an earlier sea fencible company which had been under the command of Captain John Gill, a former militia officer.[80] In November 1813, Gill received his appointment, and on February 18, reported for duty at Fort McHenry.[81] On January 29, 1814, the *Niles' Weekly Register* noted that Captain Gill had recruited

. . . a company consisting of 104 non-commissioned officers and privates, in *twenty-nine days*. We believe this company, with another that is raising, is to be in some degree attached to the flotilla designed for the defense of the upper part of the Chesapeake Bay.[82]

Earlier, Joshua Barney had been instructed by the navy secretary to "push the recruiting service as fast as possible."[83] The recruitment for the flotilla had been adversely affected by the recruiting of the Sea Fencibles as well as the Marine Artillery under Captain Stiles. In February, to help improve recruitment for the flotilla, Barney advised both the war and navy departments that, in his opinion, the sea fencibles could be transferred to his corps to act as marines. Barney had earlier noted that he "could easily manage the matter if it was not that the officers were mostly landsmen."[84]

Captain Bunbury was evidently disturbed by the commodore's proposal and wrote to the secretary of war on March 8.

> . . . I percieved that he had given you wrong information respecting our corps. He wants men and it appears that he don't mind injuring any man's feelings providing he could get them. I hope my corps will do honor to this Country should they have an opportunity of distinguishing themselves.[85]

The War Department therefore informed Major Armistead that both Sea Fencible corps were to continue their services under his command.[86]

Soon after Captain Gill had reported to Fort McHenry on February 18, Major Armistead was redirected by the War Department to order Gill's command to Fort Covington "to be put on duty and drill under Major George Keyser."[87] Major Keyser, commanding the Thirty-Eighth U. S. Infantry requested from the War Department "arms and accoutrements to prepare them for [musket] drill."[88] However, on March 17, the U. S. Senate rejected Captain Gill's appointment and relieved him of his command.[89] The command was reassigned to William Addison, and on May 9, Addison reported to Major Armistead for duty.[90]

On June 23, Major Keyser's Second Battalion of two hundred sixty men left Baltimore for Annapolis, then to St. Leonard's Town, St. Mary's County, to help defend the Patuxent River region, and to cooperate with Joshua Barney's flotilla.[91]

The organization of the Sea Fencibles was peculiar to this corps, since the legislation was derived from both U. S. navy and army regulations. Each company was to consist of one captain, one first lieutenant, one second lieutenant, one third lieutenant, one boatswain, six gunners, six quarter gunners, and ninety enlisted men. By law, the military allowances of the commissioned officers (captain and lieutenants) were derived from the army, while the boatswain, gunners, and privates received their allowances from the navy.[92] In April 1814, two hundred fifty American muskets with accoutrements were received at Fort McHenry, in order that the Sea Fencibles could assume the duties of the garrison.[93]

For the remainder of the summer of 1814, both companies performed various duties in constructing fortifications, maintaining the mast-chain boom across the harbor, and drilling in the use of musket and cannon. On June 20, Major General Samuel Smith wrote to Major Armistead and requested the following duties be assigned to the corps.

> Sir, The vicinity of the enemy makes precaution necessary. I therefore submit to your consideration the propriety of locking the booms nightly and opening them in the morning and prohibiting all vessels from going in or out after sunset. I ask leave to recommend your taking possession of the City Barges and practicing your sea fencibles to the use of them. It may soon be necessary to row guard below the fort.[94]

4 ☆ ☆ ☆ ☆

Salutes and Huzzas: The USS *Java*

The USS *Java*, rated to carry forty-four guns, dominated the shoreline of Fell's Point at the Naval Yard of Flannagain and Parsons. Supported by long sturdy hand-hewed timbers, she rested majestically on her keel of oak, ready for launch.

James Beatty, the U. S. naval agent in Baltimore, had received from the Navy Department the "necessary instructions for everything preparatory to the launch, at which the usual entertainment will be allowed . . ."[1] Among the citizens who awaited the launch was John Murray, a free black ship's caulker. Born in Baltimore nearly sixty-three years before, he had been a caulker to shipbuilders since the inception of that craft on the Point. His well-known self-attained skill in playing a "few imperfect tunes" on the violin had earned him the name of Fiddler Jack.[2]

The Naval Yard was bounded by Fountain and Fleet streets, and it was here that the *Java*'s first commander, twenty-eight-year-old Commodore Oliver H. Perry, had been ordered on July 17, 1814.[3] The occasion of her launching on August 1 was described by a correspondent of the *Baltimore Patriot*.

LAUNCH!

The Frigate *Java*, whose name reminds us of the glorious deeds of one of our naval heroes, and which is to be, we trust, the theatre of new exploits, by another who has already insured imperishable fame, was launched this morning, at the Navy yard, pursuant to previous notice. We will not emulate, since we cannot equal, the lofty strains, in which some of our Boston brethren announced affairs of their description. We merely state that she moved into her "destined element" (as the phrase is) in a very handsome stile, amidst general and joyful cheers; that a very numerous assemblage of ladies and gentlemen attended; that salutes were fired by the Marine Artillery, by other Artillery companies of the city, by the *U. S. Barges* and by Infantry; that on board the Sloop of War *Erie*, which layed at a commodious distance, the Yager Band of Music enliven the scene with appropriate marches and airs; and that her appearance was universally admired. She is thought to be one of the finest vessels that ever floated, and as such is worthy the command of the Hero of Lake Erie.[4]

The *Niles' Weekly Register* commented that

. . . she reached her element in great stile, and was hartily greeted with salutes and hazzas . . . She is like an article of cabinet work; and every piece of timber was carefully selected. Her rate is of 44 guns . . .[5]

At 9 A.M., she was launched in the elegant naval tradition of her day. Her signal pennants flew, while, in the background, the reverberating salutes of artillery filled the harbor basin where nearly twenty thousand spectators had gathered for the occasion. Not since 1797, when the U. S. Frigate *Constellation* was launched at David Stoddard's shipyard on nearby Harris Creek, had there been such an assemblage of citizen spirit.

The skilled craftsmen who built the *Java*, and those who cheered her at this moment, were unaware of other frigates and ships of war that were now moving under a full press of canvas toward the Chesapeake from the British naval base in Bermuda. The festive spirit subsided as the war clouds approached Baltimore harbor.

5 ☆ ☆ ☆ ☆ ☆

CONFLAGRATION AT WASHINGTON

On August 1, 1814, the HMS *Tonnant*, 80 guns, hoisted sail with a squadron of ships of war and slowly cleared the coral reef harbor of St. George, Bermuda, heading for the waters of the Chesapeake Bay. From her top foremast flew the white flag of fifty-six-year-old Vice Admiral Sir Alexander Cochrane, Knight of the Bath, and newly appointed commander in chief of the North American Station. Cochrane had received orders to take the forces under his command "in such operations as may be found best calculated for the advantage of His Majesty's Service, and the annoyance of the enemy."[1]

Joining the Vice Admiral was Major General Robert Ross, forty-seven years old, a veteran of the Iberian Peninsula Campaign and recently appointed to command the expeditionary forces that were to accompany Cochrane.[2] His instructions by British War Secretary Earl Bathurst were quite definite in setting forth his role relative to that of the Vice Admiral; Ross had authority to "freely express" his opinions with "veto power" concerning the military deployment of the troops and, once ashore, had overall command of the land forces.[3]

On the afternoon of August 14, HMS *Tonnant*, commanded by Captain John Wainwright, arrived at the mouth of the Potomac River and dropped anchor. Awaiting the Vice Admiral's arrival with his own squadron was Rear Admiral George Cockburn, on board HMS *Albion*, 74 guns. A skillful naval tactician, Cockburn had obtained the noted distinction of being the most hated British officer on the Chesapeake tidewater.

Earlier in the summer, in a dispatch of July 17, Cockburn assured Cochrane, the new commander in chief, of the objective:

> . . . I feel no hesitation in stating to you that I consider the town of Benedict in the Patuxent, to offer us the advantages for the purpose beyond any other spot in the United States . . . within forty-eight hours after the arrival in the Patuxent of such a force as you expect, the City of Washington might be possessed without any difficulty or opposition of any kind . . .[4]

On the evening of August 14, a conference was held within the vice admiral's cabin for the planned joint naval and military offensive against the city of Washington, if the situation proved favorable. On the evening of the sixteenth, the main troop convoy of twenty-four vessels arrived, the blue pennant of Rear Admiral Poultney Malcolm flying from HMS *Royal Oak*, 74 guns, as she was saluted with naval artillery. The expeditionary forces that accompanied Malcolm were veteran troops consisting of the Fourth Regiment, King's Own; the Twenty-First Regiment, Royal North British Fusileers; the Forty-Fourth Regiment, East Essex; and the Eighty-Fifth Regiment (Bucks Volunteers) of Light Infantry, a total of 3,714 soldiers. Combined with the marines and seamen of the Royal Navy, an estimated force of 5,000 seasoned veterans were ready to chastise the Americans.[5]

During a final briefing the next morning, the captains of the fleet received the tentative outline of the campaign. By the afternoon of the seventeenth, the fleet weighed anchor and made sail. The three naval squadrons consisted of nearly fifty ships of war. Attached were four divisions of troop launches, a total of eighty.[6] A young British midshipman, Robert Barrett, stationed aboard HMS *Hebrus*, 38 guns, viewed their departure:

> . . . It was a glorious and imposing spectacle to behold these noble ships standing up the vast bay of the Chesapeake, into the very heart of America; manned, too, with eager souls, panting for fame . . . the flags of three British Admirals, Cochrane, Cockburn, and Poultney Malcolm, were proudly flying at the mastheads of their respective vessels, the *Tonnant*, *Albion*, and *Royal Oak* . . . Here was a splendid array of gallant and meritorious

officers whose skill and bravery were conspiciously registered in
the annals of fame . . .[7]

The main squadron carrying the expeditionary forces under
Cockburn and Ross proceeded up the Patuxent River with the hope
of destroying Joshua Barney's Chespeake Flotilla, and then marching
directly overland to the American capital. Captain James Alexander
Gordon, of HMS *Seahorse*, 38 guns, led a diversion up the Potomac
River. His orders were

> . . . to take under your orders the ships named in the margin
> [*Euryalus, Devastation, Etna, Terror, Manly,* and the *Erebus*] &
> proceed therewith up the Potomac River as high as you may find
> practicable without endangering the ships for the purpose of
> keeping the country bordering the river in a state of alarm and to
> bombard and destroy if possible such fortifications as the enemy
> may have erected for the protection of its navigation . . .[8]

A second diversion was added to Cockburn's plan. A small squadron under Captain Peter Parker, aboard HMS *Menelaus*, 36 guns,
was to proceed

> . . . to the upper part of the Chespeake Bay above Baltimore, for
> the purpose of cutting off, all water communications between that
> place & Elk Town & generally to threaten & annoy the enemy in
> that quarter . . .[9]

On the morning of the seventeenth, Cochrane's invasion fleet
sailed up the Chesapeake under a fair wind. The three squadrons
departed for their assignments; Parker continuing northward, Gordon
up the Potomac, while Cockburn and Cochrane entered the Patuxent
with the expeditionary forces.

However, it was not until the morning of the nineteenth that
word reached Commodore Barney at Nottingham, about thirty miles
upstream. At 9 A.M., Barney sent word to the secretary of the navy
indicating that a large force of some forty vessels was standing up the
Patuxent for Benedict, Maryland, with a determination to go to
Washington, where, the Rear Admiral said, "he would dine . . . on
Sunday after having destroyed the Flotilla . . ."[10]

The British intention was certainly directed toward Barney's flotilla.
More attractive, however, were the warehouses and naval yards of

Baltimore, the nation's third largest city. Notwithstanding, a powerful expeditionary force was clearly threatening the capital. Secretary
of the Navy William Jones, upon receipt of Barney's dispatch, sent
couriers to Commodore John Rodgers in Philadelphia and Captain
David Porter in New York. To Rodgers, the secretary wrote:

> Sir, The enemy has entered the Patuxent with a very large force,
> indicating a design upon this place, which may be real, or it may
> serve to mask his design upon Baltimore. In either case it is
> exceedingly desirable to collect in our vicinity all the disposable
> force within reach as soon as possible. You will therefore with the
> least possible delay proceed to Baltimore with about 300 men
> (including officers) of the force under your command and also
> order on the detachment of Marines from Cecil Furnace to meet
> you in Baltimore where the further orders of the Department will
> await you.[11]

Porter collected the remains of the crew of the U. S. Frigate *Essex*
with the following summons in New York.

> FREE TRADE AND SAILOR'S RIGHTS—to the crew of the old *Essex*.
> SAILORS, the enemy is about attempting the destruction of your
> new ship at Washington, & I am ordered there to defend her. I
> shall proceed immediately, & all disposed to accompany me will
> meet me at 5 o'clock this afternoon at the navy agent's office.[12]

Porter received the secretary's letter on the twenty-third and
ordered a detachment of U. S. Marines under Lieutenant Samuel
Johnson to depart, to be followed later by the commodore.[13] Rodgers
immediately gathered the officers and seamen of the U. S. Frigate
Guerriere and proceeded south to the Susquehanna River. At Havre
de Grace, Maryland, Rodgers was joined by Lieutenant Joseph
Kuhn's U. S. Marine detachment from the *Guerriere*. With twenty-
five wagons, Rodgers's force of three hundred fifty men made haste
for Baltimore.[14]

In the meantime, events were unfolding rapidly in Baltimore and on
the Patuxent. Major General Samuel Smith had received orders from
the president to bring into federal service the Third Brigade of the
Maryland Militia. Smith issued his division orders on August 19,

. . . Therefore ordered, that the whole brigade be held in readiness for *actual service,* that they parade at 4 o'clock *this day,* completely armed and equipped. The quarter masters of the respective regiments will draw cartridges, and every box will be filled upon the ground. The men for the present will quarter at their respective homes. The reveille will beat at gun firing every morning; when the regiments will assemble and train by regiment until 8 o'clock; they will again assemble at 4 o'clock, and train until seven o'clock.

On the alarm gun being fired, the regiments will meet on their respective parade grounds, and wait further orders. The third brigade is now in the pay of the United States, in service subject to the articles of war . . .[15]

While the Third Brigade paraded on Hampstead Hill (now Patterson Park), British forces were coordinating their efforts to locate and destroy the Chesapeake Flotilla, known to be in the vicinity of Nottingham, Maryland, on the Patuxent, some twenty-five miles upstream. On August 19, the British land troops under Major General Robert Ross landed unopposed at Benedict. Midshipman Barrett wrote:

. . . The charming little village of Benedict is one of the most sequestered and lovely hamlets in existance; it is situated on the left bank of the Patuxent (from the sea), about forty miles distant from the mouth of the river, (as near as I could guess,) and was selected for the landing-place, because a road proceeded from thence to Nottingham and Washington . . .[16]

The next day the British started their march toward Nottingham. From the deck of HMS *Hebrus,* anchored offshore, Midshipman Barrett described the departure of his comrades:

. . . The 20th of August proved to be a stirring day; for the army proceeded on their march, whilst a numerous flotilla of boats, well armed, and formed in three divisions, under the command of Rear-Admiral Cockburn, ascended the river in quest of Commodore Barney's seventeen gun-boats, which were supposed to be at least thirty or forty miles distant; and, in consequence of this movement, it will at once be perceived that, as the route which the army pursued was parallel to the river, of course their right flank was protected, and they could easily communicate with this powerful armament. Never, in the whole course of my life, have I since witnessed a more imposing spectacle than the numerous tenders, launches, barges, and cutters of the fleet presented, with their colours gaily streaming, whilst the sun glistened on their various fancy sails and the uniforms of the Royal Marines . . .[17]

As the British army marched in the August heat toward Nottingham, Brigadier General William Winder began to mobilize the American forces near Washington. Captured on the Canadian frontier in 1813, the thirty-nine-year-old Winder had recently been released. Upon his return, the president appointed him (on July 2) commander of the new Tenth Military District, which consisted of the state of Maryland, northern Virginia (between the Rappahannock and Potomac rivers), and the District of Columbia. Emory Upton in the classic *The Military Policy of the United States*, states:

> . . . The command of the new District was devolved upon General Winder, whose selection, according to the statement of the Secretary of War, was based "not on the ground of distinguished professional service or knowledge," but simply on a presumption that, "being a native of Maryland and a relative of the governor, Brigadier Winder would be useful in mitigating the opposition to the war, and in giving an increased efficiency to national measures within the limits of the State.[18]

Reinforcements of militia and federal troops were arriving to counter the enemy's movement, wherever it might develop. Winder soon discovered that his new command was a political "paper army."[19] Earlier, Winder had strongly advised the War Department that a portion of the Maryland quota of the militia forces be stationed between Baltimore and Washington for their mutual protection.[20] The secretary responded "that the most advantageous mode of using militia was upon the spur of the occasion, and to bring them to fight as soon as called out [into federal service]."[21]

General Winder spent the summer of 1814 inspecting fortifications. Unfortunately, by August, he had nothing to show for his defense measures because of political circumstances in Washington. In response to Major General John P. Van Ness, commander of the

District of Columbia's militia and advocate of stronger defense measures for the capital, Secretary Armstrong informed him on August 19, "Oh, yes! By God, they would not come with such a fleet without meaning to strike somewhere, but they certainly will not come here; what the devil will they do here?"[22]

While Winder waited for orders to march, the British army was already moving toward Nottingham. Lieutenant Colonel Franklin Wharton, Commandant of the Marine Corps, received orders from the Navy Department to gather the one hundred twenty marines under Captain Samuel Miller and rendezvous with Commodore Barney on the Patuxent. The commandant replied they would be ready to march on the twenty-first.[23] Barney was directed to employ the marines as infantry and include them under his command, subject to the orders of General Winder.[24]

General Ross's strategy once he reached Nottingham was still uncertain, though the capital was clearly within his grasp. He could turn westward, attack Fort Washington, then move on to Washington with the aid of Captain Gordon's flotilla. Secretary Jones expressed his opinion that certainly the America flotilla was a worthy goal for the British, however, "It may be a feint to mask a real design on Baltimore," he informed Barney.[25]

At 2 A.M., on the twentieth, General Winder moved his army from Washington across the Eastern Branch (Anacostia River) of the Potomac into the Maryland countryside. Proceeding along the Upper Marlboro Road, he reached Wood Yard (a small crossroads) on the afternoon of the twenty-first.[26]

Secretary of State James Monroe, who had been riding in the Patuxent countryside, rode into Winder's encampment to report that the British had occupied Nottingham. Throughout the day, Winder received reinforcements. From as far away as Carlisle, Pennsylvania, Lieutenant Colonel Jacint Laval's company of 125 dragoons arrived, 300 men from the Thirty-Eighth U. S. Infantry, and militia detachments. From the Washington Navy Yard, Captain Miller's U. S. Marines had finally arrived with three 12-pounders and two long 18-pound field guns.[27] Winder's army now began to show some promise as a defensive force, with an artillery park of some twenty field guns.[28]

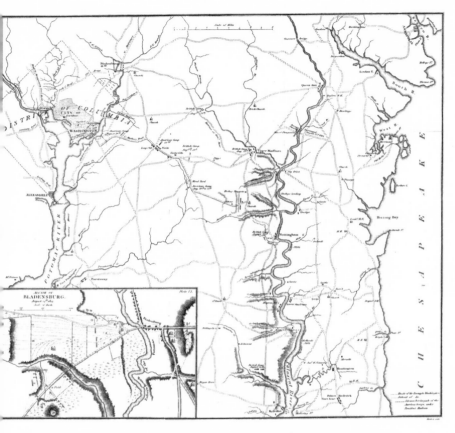

"Advance of the British Column, from Benedict, on the Patuxent River, to the City of Washington, August 1814." From William M. James: *Military Occurances*, London, 1818.

As the American army settled in for the night, Winder planned the next movement for his inexperienced and ill-disciplined collection of regulars and militia. At 10 P.M., Winder sent off a dispatch to Brigadier General Tobias Stansbury and Lieutenant Colonel Joseph Sterett, who were marching from Baltimore with 1,350 militia artillery and infantry to halt at Bladensburg.[29]

The general defensive plan for the Americans was still uncertain. Where in the wooded countryside to the east was General Ross? No

artillery engagements had been heard to pinpoint their location. In
the early morning hours of August 22, General Winder decided to
take the offensive. At 2 A.M., the company drums sounded reveille,
calling the troops to parade for inspection. By sunrise, the American
army proceeded toward Nottingham with Winder and James Monroe
scouting ahead. Five miles down the Wood Yard Road, they rode into
the farmyard of Benjamin Oden, located within sight of two strategic
crossroads.[30]

The junction was a deciding factor as to what direction and objective
the British would ultimately pursue. One road led west to the Wood
Yard, the other northward toward Upper Marlboro, located within a
day's march of the capital. Winder immediately sent forward a detachment of Lieutenant Colonel Laval's dragoons to scout the enemy's advance along the road from Nottingham. Within half an hour,
the dragoons returned to the Oden farmyard. Laval reported that
they had encountered Ross's army at the crossroads, bearing in the
direction of the Americans.

Observing the British advance, James Monroe hastily sent a
message to the president in Washington:

> . . . The enemy are advanced six miles on the road to the Wood
> Yard, and our troops retiring. Our troops were on the march to
> meet them, but in too small a body to engage. General Winder
> proposes to retire till he can collect them in a body. The enemy
> are in full march for Washington . . . You had better remove the
> [public] records . . .[31]

Ross had briefly encountered the vanguard of the American cavalry along the road, unaware of the main American army ahead of him.
Believing the dragoons to be only a reconnaissance detachment, he
reversed his line of march and took the road north toward Upper
Marlboro. The orders from Lord Bathurst in London had been quite
clear, Ross was "not to engage in any extended operations at a
distance from the coast."[32] In truth, Ross was already nearly twenty
miles from the British fleet at Benedict, and four or five miles from
the Patuxent, where Admiral Cockburn was sailing hard upon the
American flotilla.

The commodore had sailed his Chesapeake Flotilla up the Patuxent
and reached the vicinity of Pig Point on the evening of the twenty-

first. There the shallow water prevented any further navigation. Barney's orders were to destroy the flotilla to prevent its capture, and then join General Winder.[33] Reluctantly, Barney departed the flotilla with four hundred men of his command. His final order to Lieutenant Solomon Frazier, left behind with a detachment, was to set fire to the flotilla when the enemy appeared. Having given the order, the commodore marched with his force toward Upper Marlboro and spent the night.[34] After several months of service to the country, Barney's flotilla of barges now waited for its own inevitable denouement—a final confrontation with Rear Admiral George Cockburn.

On the morning of the twenty-second, as General Ross continued northward, the Rear Admiral began his search for the American flotilla, which he knew to be not far upstream. The British seamen's enthusiasm was high at the prospect of engaging the wily American commodore. At 11 A.M., the American flotilla was sighted at Pig Point. In his official account, Cockburn noted the scene that unfolded before the British tars:

> . . . Our boats now advanced towards them as rapidly as possible, but on nearing them we observed the sloop bearing the broad pennant to be on fire, and she very soon afterwards blew up. I now saw clearly that they were all abandoned and on fire with trains to their magazines, and out of the seventeen vessels which composed this formidable and so much vaunted flotilla sixteen were in quick succession blown to atoms, and the seventeenth, in which the fire had not taken, was captured. The commodore's sloop was a large armed vessel, the others were gun boats all having a long gun in the bow and a carronade in the stern, but the calibre of the guns and the number of the crew of each differed in proportion to the size of the boat, varying from 32 pdrs. and 60 men, to 18 pdrs. and 40 men. I found here laying above the flotilla under its protection thirteen merchant schooners, some of which not being worth bringing away I caused to be burnt, such as were in good condition, I directed to be moved to Pig Point. Whilst employed taking these vessels a few shots were fired at us by some of the men of the flotilla from the bushes on the shore near us, but Lieutenant Scott whom I landed for that purpose, soon got hold of them and made them prisoners. Some horsemen likewise shewed themselves on the neighbouring heights, but a rocket or two

depended them without resistance. Now spreading his men
through the country, the enemy retreated to a distance and left us
in quiet possession of the town, the neighbourhood, and our
prizes . . .[35]

Lieutenant Frazier had done his duty and fled ashore to join the
commodore, who, undoubtedly, heard the explosions as the flotilla
was blown apart and scuttled.[36] Soon thereafter, Barney found
Winder's army retiring toward Washington. The commodore was
astounded at Winder's lack of good military judgment, by not taking a
defensive position. Winder replied that his intention was to place the
American army between the capital and the enemy. Black flotillaman
Charles Ball expressed his opinion in a narrative published years
later:

> . . . I marched with the troops of Barney . . . through heavy
> forests of timber, or numerous and dense cedar thickets. It is my
> opinion, that if General Winder had marched the half of the
> troops that he had at Bladensburg, down to the lower part of
> Prince George county, and attacked the British in these woods
> and cedar thickets, not a man of them would ever have reached
> Bladensburg. I feel confident that in the country through which I
> marched, one hundred Americans would have destroyed a thou-
> sand of the enemy, by falling trees across the road, and attacking
> them in ambush . . .[37]

With the destruction of Barney's flotilla and his right flank secured, Major General Ross encamped early that afternoon at the
small town of Upper Marlboro, situated on the western branch of the
Patuxent River. As his field headquarters, Ross selected the home of
sixty-five-year-old Dr. William Beanes, a prominent physician and
landowner. Lieutenant George R. Gleig of the Eighty-Fifth Foot
wrote:

> . . . The doctor was, in point of fact, a Scotchman; that is to say,
> he had migrated about twenty years ago from some district of
> North Britain, and still retained his native dialect in all its doric
> richness. He professed, moreover, to retain the feelings as well as
> the language of his boyish days. He was a Federalist—in other
> words, he was hostile to the war with England, which he still
> persisted in regarding as his mother country. Such, at least, were
> the statements with which he favoured us, and we believed him

the more readily, that he seemed really disposed to treat us as friends. There was nothing about his house or farm to which he made us not heartily welcome; and the wily emigrant was no loser by his civility . . .³⁸

The British army was now some thirty miles from the fleet at Benedict. Lacking cavalry and artillery, Ross began to feel some uncertainty about whether to continue to push forward with the Rear Admiral's plan or to return to the fleet. He had extended the campaign so far without any real resistance from the Americans. His junior officers urged him to push on toward Washington—only sixteen miles away. To help sway the general's indecision, two members of his staff returned to the Patuxent to solicit Cockburn's aid.³⁹

At the American encampment at Long Old Fields, eight miles east of the capital, Winder was in conference with the president, the naval secretary, and Barney. From this new defensive position, the Americans could easily pivot northward to Bladensburg, or southward to Fort Washington on the Potomac.

Early on the morning of the twenty-third, the persuasive Admiral Cockburn disembarked from his vessel and rode four miles in the night to confer and cajole the major general back into line. Deputy-Quartermaster Lieutenant George De Lacy Evans, a young, twenty-three-year-old officer on Ross's staff, felt that a crucial moment in Cockburn's plan was about to be dashed by Ross's indecisiveness. The army was so close to the American capital that a quick movement would be necessary before any firm resistance could be mustered by the Americans. Time was of the utmost importance. Any delay could ruin their perfect opportunity to strike a demoralizing blow to the heart of these "upstart Americans."⁴⁰

The decision was made. At 2 P.M., detachments from the Royal Navy joined the British army, and leaving Upper Marlboro and their amiable host, Dr. William Beanes, behind, they marched toward the capital of the United States. While the British expeditionary forces continued through the Maryland countryside, life aboard HMS *Hebrus* anchored at Benedict remained peacefully secluded. Midshipman Robert Barrett explained in his narrative:

. . . From the period that Nottingham and Pig Point had been captured, we were continually employed on board clearing the numerous launches and barges which arrived at all hours laden with vast hogsheads of tobacco; most of these boats had landed occasionally in their passage down to procure poultry and sheep (the quarters of which decorated their sterns), which served to ensure Jack a good bellyful, as some little recompense for his hard and toilsome labour under the rays of a scorching sun . . . If our men wanted tobacco, a boat was sent ashore to get as much from the racks of a neighbouring store as she could contain; then, on coming alongside, the boatswain or his mate would pipe "All hands on deck for tobacco, ahoy!" when the men went down and helped themselves freely to what they wanted, and the rest was flung overboard. When will Jack ever see such times again! . . .[41]

Thomas Kennedy, an American scout, had been keeping a close watch on the British camp at Upper Marlboro all morning. He noticed activity in the camp—perhaps in preparation to attack within the day. Secretary of War John Armstrong on receiving word replied, "They are foraging, I suppose; and if an attack is meditated by them upon any place, it is Annapolis."[42] Winder took the offensive and decided to attack.

With militia reinforcements arriving from Baltimore, Winder rode to Bladensburg to confer with the officers on the situation. To locate the movements of the British, a detachment proceeded eastward toward Upper Marlboro.[43] Shortly after 2 P.M., gunfire disrupted the tranquil, rolling landscape. The American detachment had encountered the entire British army on the march. The Americans immediately formed a defensive line across the road leading to the American encampment. Commodore Barney drew up his flotillamen, flanked by two battalions of the Thirty-Sixth and Thirty-Eighth U. S. Infantry.[44] When word reached Winder, his hopes of leading an early morning offensive the next day were now all but scrapped. It was, however, late afternoon and darkness would soon render artillery less than helpful. Not more than four miles away, the veteran British army was closing rapidly on the Americans. As for Winder's own army, with the exception of the marines and Barney's flotillamen, they were wholly unprepared for a general assault at night. To avoid a fearful demoralized rout of his militia, Winder ordered a retreat to Washington arriving that evening.[45]

Confident of the American's reluctance to engage, the British encamped for the night. In the early morning hours of August 24, Admiral Cockburn's aide, Lieutenant James Scott, arrived from Benedict with a message from Cochrane. In a word, Cochrane expressed disapproval of an attack. The army had accomplished more than had been expected. The vice admiral now expressed a desire for their return.[46]

Cockburn was shaken. They were so close to putting the final touch on the plan he had personally initiated. Showing the message to Ross, Cockburn addressed the veteran commander in his own articulate and persuasive manner. Finally, Ross gave in to the elder Cockburn's wishes, and at 5 A.M., the British broke camp and renewed their march for the nation's capital.

Winder had been up nearly the entire night, checking on the precautionary measures to destroy the two bridges leading to the District and the safety of the Navy Yard.[47] By dawn, he was back in camp, fatigued and inconsolable. Since his appointment as commander of the military district, the administration had virtually washed its hands of the whole question of a defensive strategy. The War Department had failed to offer any adequate military assistance to discipline the militia quota of troops assigned to him. He also remembered John Armstrong's remark a few days earlier about using militia "upon the spur of the occasion."[48] In all, it was a situation of utter despair. Winder could only attempt to do his best under the circumstances. Perhaps, by some lucky turn of events, the British would return to the Patuxent. However, by 9 A.M., reconnaissance reported the British were pressing toward the city. Shortly after 10 A.M., the British, now only two miles beyond Old Fields, made an unexpected feint northward towards Bladensburg, forcing Winder to reshuffle his defensive lines.[49]

Lieutenant George Gleig, advancing with the Eighty-Fifth Foot, continued his narrative of the campaign:

> . . . the hour of noon was past, when our attention was suddenly drawn to the left, by several heavy clouds of dust which rose in that direction. Though we could not doubt from what source the dust proceeded, the intervention of a considerable copse between us and it, hindered us from saying with certainty that the

enemy was in the position. The screen thus interposed was, however, speedily withdrawn. A farther advance of some hundred and fifty yards brought us clear of the plantation, and the American army became visible . . . The corps which occupied the heights above Bladensburg, was composed chiefly of militia; and as the American militia are not dressed in uniform, it exhibited to our eyes a very singular, and a very awkward appearance . . . I have seldom been more forcibly struck with anything than with the contrast, which a glance to the rear afforded at this moment, with the spectacle which was before me. A column of four thousand British soldiers, moving in sections of six abreast, and covering an extent of road greater than its windings would permit the eye to take in, met my gaze in that quarter . . .[50]

The ensuing Battle of Bladensburg, which has been provided in detail in numerous accounts, was one of the darkest moments in American military history. Narrative eyewitness accounts, from both sides, however, attest to the heroic stand made by Commodore Barney's command. The following excerpt from Barney's official report to the navy secretary best explains the role of the U. S. marines and his own flotillamen:

. . . When I arrived at the line, which separates the District from Maryland, the battle began . . . We took our position on the rising ground, put the pieces in battery, posted the Marines under Capt. Miller, and the flotilla men who were to act as infantry under their own officers, on my right, to support the pieces & waited the approach of the enemy.

During this period the engagement continued—the enemy advancing and our army retreating before them, apparently in much disorder . . . in a few minutes the enemy again advanced, when I ordered the 18-pounders to be fired, which completely cleared the road; shortly after, a second and third attempt was made by the enemy to come forward, but all who made the attempt was destroyed . . . By this time not a vestige of the American army remained except a body of five or six hundred posted on a height on my right from whom I expected much support from their fine situation . . . who to my great mortification made no resistance, giving a fire or two and retiring . . . In this situation we had the whole army of the enemy to contend with; our ammunition was expended, and unfortunately the drivers of my ammunition wagons had gone off in the general panic. Capt. Miller was wounded . . . At this time I received a severe wound in my thigh. Finding the enemy now completely in our rear and no means of defense, I gave the orders to my officers and men to retire . . .[51]

Black flotillaman Charles Ball viewed the incoming redcoats from his position with the flotilla guns:

. . . I stood by my gun, until the Commodore was shot down, when he ordered us to retreat, as I was told by the officer who commanded our gun. If the militia regiments, that lay upon our right and left, could have been brought to charge the British, in close fight, as they crossed the bridge, we should have killed or taken the whole of them in a short time; but the militia ran like sheep, chased by dogs . . .[52]

Barney soon came face-to-face with his British adversaries, whom he had skillfully managed to elude those past few hectic days. General Ross immediately paroled the commodore, had his wound dressed, and later allowed him to recuperate at his own home. Barney was placed under the care of Captain Wainwright of the *Tonnant*, while Ross and Cockburn attended to the business at hand.

At 8 P.M., the British army entered the American capital, now virtually deserted. Many of the government buildings were set afire. The Navy Yard went up in flames at 8:20, set afire at the last moment by departing U. S. naval personnel. Around 10 o'clock, the Capitol burst into flames, soon followed by the President's House, adding to the awful yet blazing grandeur of the night.[53]

The conflagration at Washington could be seen from miles away. Down the Potomac River, a British officer on board the bomb vessel *Meteor*, advancing slowly up river with Gordon's flotilla, noted in the ship's log, "Saw a large fire, NNW."[54] At Baltimore, nearly forty miles away, a sense of acute trepidation consumed the citizens who had gathered upon Federal Hill. Looking toward the horizon, in the direction of Washington, the fiery glow awakened concern among the Baltimoreans. At Fort McHenry, militia Private Benjamin Cohen also witnessed the view from the ramparts of the Star Fort.[55]

On the evening of the twenty-fifth, amidst a severe summer thunderstorm, the British army withdrew and retraced their steps

back to Benedict, arriving on the twenty-eighth. Behind them on
Pennsylvania Avenue lay strewn the contents of the *National Intelligencer* office. Ironically, an editorial comment on the morning of the
twenty-fourth read, "We feel assured that the numbers and bravery
of our men will afford complete protection to the city."[56]

As the British retired to their transports, the remnants of the
Baltimore militia under Brigadier General Tobias Stansbury and
Lieutenant Colonel Joseph Sterett began their return to Baltimore. A
Marylander who had fought at Bladensburg wrote of the despair he
found in Baltimore upon his return.

> But to my sorrow it is not to end here. We expect every instant to
> hear that they have taken up the line of march for this place and if
> they do we are gone.[57]

The news, to say the least, was unbelievable. How could the nation's
capital have been left so unprepared? Would the city of Baltimore
share the same fate? The questions were many, but few qualified
answers were available to calm the citizenry of Baltimore.

As the events that led to the Battle of Bladensburg unfolded,
Major General Samuel Smith continued to strengthen and organize
the defenses of Baltimore. On August 16, in a letter to the governor of
Maryland, Smith wrote:

> . . . A Company of Mariners under the title of the First Marine
> Artillery of the Union has been formed and have selected their
> officers . . . composed of more than 100 men principally mari-
> ners . . . I consider them a most important corps . . . The U. S.
> have lent them four 18-pounders on traveling carriages which
> they have [put] in fine order . . .[58]

Smith requested commissaries for acquiring the necessary supplies for the Corps of Seamen. Stationed at Fort McHenry and
Battery Babcock, they were now, following the American defeat at
Bladensburg, ordered to Hampstead Hill, a military ploy to improve
the city's morale.

The muster roll of the Corps of Seamen listed many of Baltimore's
most prominent sea captains. In the first year of the war they had so
effectively raided and destroyed part of Britain's merchant fleet as to
cause the Admiralty to look upon Baltimore with distaste. In the
ranks were Sergeant Pearl Durkee and Private William Wade, late

commanders of the *Chasseur*. This famous Baltimore-built privateer schooner was now sailing under the command of Thomas Boyle. At that moment the *Chasseur* was cruising the British coastline, and issued a proclamation that was posted at Lloyd's Coffee House in London. Boyle's tongue-in-cheek proclamation read in part:

> Whereas it has been customary with the Admirals of Great Britain commanding the small forces on the coast of the United States . . . to declare the coast of the said United States, in a state of strict, and rigorous blockade . . . I do therefore, by virtue of the Power and Authority in me vested (possessing sufficient force) declare all the Ports, Harbours, Bays, Creeks, Rivers, Inlets, Outlets, Islands, and Sea Coast of the United Kingdom of Great Britain and Ireland in a state of strict and rigorous Blockade . . .[59]

Despite the inability of several British warships to capture the bold and elusive Yankee captain of this single American privateer, their counterparts in America had accomplished a great deal. In six days, since their landing at Benedict, the British had forced the destruction of Barney's flotilla, defeated the American army, captured the capital, and acquired or destroyed large quantities of military hardware and domestic farm products.

Four days after Bladensburg, Naval Secretary William Jones wrote to Commodore John Rodgers, who had arrived in Baltimore on the twenty-fifth:

> . . . Had it been possible for your force to have participated in the action at Bladensburg, you would have had the glory of saving the capital. For undoubtedly you would have turned the scale which was for some time balanced until the want of discipline more than the merit of the enemy turned it in his favor . . .[60]

6 ☆ ☆ ☆ ☆ ☆

THE MARITIME DEFENSE
OF BALTIMORE

On Tuesday, August 30, 1814, at 1 P.M., as a result of the crises that enveloped Baltimore, George Douglass joined with his fellow merchants as a private in Captain Joseph Nicholson's militia company of the Baltimore Fencibles. To his friend Henry Wheaton, editor of the *National Advocate* in New York, Douglass wrote:

> . . . Every American heart is bursting with shame and indignation at the catastophe [at Washington]. The people of Baltimore were at first surprized and confounded and expected at any moment to be attacked, not knowing the real strength of the enemy, but the agony is past, the panic dissipated, and they now appear as they ought always to have been.
>
> We have recovered from our consternation. All hearts and hands have cordially united in the common cause. Everyday, almost every hour, bodies of troops are marching in to our assistance. At this moment we cannot have less than 10,000 men under arms. The whole of the hills and rising grounds to the eastward of the port are covered with horse-foot and artillery exercises and training from morning until night.
>
> They present an extensive and beautiful prospect of a multitude of tents, baggage, and cannon in every direction. Last Sunday, at least a mile of entrenchments with suitable batteries were raised as if by magic, at which are now working all sorts of people, old and young, white and black, in so much, before Saturday next

we expect that every vulnerable point will be strongly fortified.

Captain George Stiles made a distinguished figure in those noble exertions. Already we feel confident of our safety, and of beating the enemy if he does attack us. The horrible mismanagement at Washington has taught us a useful lesson, and we must be worse than stupid if we do not make proper use of it. We have hearts and hands in abundance and all we want is *heads* to conduct us. Make what you can of the above, you may depend upon its authenticity . . .[1]

The day after Bladensburg, Baltimore Mayor Edward Johnson convened a meeting of the leading citizens in the City Council chambers. A Committee of Vigilance and Safety was formed (that replaced the earlier Committee of Public Supply) to administer the government and to organize defense efforts.[2] The Committee adopted a resolution that such members appointed,

. . . wait on Major General Smith and . . . request that he at this important crisis take upon himself the command of the forces that may be called out for the defense of our city.[3]

The Committee had received a visit from the leading military commanders within the city: Brigadier General John Stricker, commanding the Third Brigade of the Maryland Militia; Major George Armistead, Commodore Oliver H. Perry, and Captain Robert Spence, senior naval officer. Together they expressed a wish that Samuel Smith assume command.[4]

Although grateful that three well-known officers of the regular military establishment and the Committee had selected him as commander, Smith was aware of the fact that General William Winder still outranked him as commander of the Tenth Military District. Only if he had been called into federal service as a major general, would Smith outrank Winder.

Not one to let conflicting orders and the confusion of the Baltimore command repeat itself as it had in 1813 with General Miller, Smith asked for the governor's official endorsement. On the twenty-sixth, Smith received from Annapolis an endorsed copy of the vague order calling him into federal service. The governor quite simply restated the orders of a year before.

By the requisition of the President of the United States of the 4th of July last, one Major General is required of this state, in conformity to which, you have been selected.[5]

Smith lost no time in letting General Winder, who was hurrying to Baltimore to take command, know who was in charge. Smith wrote,

The endorsed copy of a letter from his Excellency Governor Winder was received by me this day, and I have in consequence assumed the command agreeable to my rank.[6]

General Winder arrived the next day and immediately confronted Smith. Winder protested that the governor had had no legal authority appointing Smith as commander. Winder had been appointed commander of the Tenth Military District, which included Baltimore, by the president, and legally he was in command.

In the days afterward, Winder continued his efforts to assume his official rank by communicating his concerns to the president, Washington officials, and to Secretary of War John Armstrong. Armstrong was in Baltimore at the home of Captain Joseph H. Nicholson, a long time political adversary of Smith. Nicholson expressed his concern in a letter to his cousin, the wife of the American Peace Commissioner, Albert Gallatin, residing in Philadelphia:

. . . Our militia are so raw, and so totally undisciplined, and our commanding General so entirely unqualified to organize them, that I have very little confidence of our success. The command has been taken from Gen'l Winder and given to Gen'l Smith. The latter assumed it in the first instance without authority, at the request of some of our citizens, and the debate has since been confined at Washington.

There is some derangement of the administration which I do not understand, Gen'l Armstrong is here, and says he is no longer Secretary of War, but everyone who comes from the city, says he is still considered so there. Mr. Madison had been waited on by a deputation from Georgetown, of whom Alexander C. Hanson [Editor of the Georgetown *Federal Republican*] was one, who told him that they would not agree to defend the place, or to make any resistance, if Gen'l Armstrong was to have control over them. That Mr. Madison in consequence of this and much other remonstrations of a simular nature, proposed to Armstrong that he should do all the business of the War Department, except that which related to the District; that Armstrong immediately answered he must do the whole business or none, and tendered his resignation [on the 29th], which was not accepted. He added, however, in his conversation with me, "I am here, and the President is in Washington . . ."[7]

The controversy ended when, on September 11, Acting Secretary of War James Monroe addressed a letter to General Winder:

. . . Gen'l Smith's command must extend to Annapolis, & to other points along the bay, to which the enemy may direct their movements . . . There can be but one commander, in every quarter, by which any particular force is intended. The force at Baltimore being relied on for the protection of that place, Annapolis & all other places in the district on the bay, being under Gen'l Smith the movement of the troops must be under his control . . .[8]

Delegated by Smith to the command of the city's western defenses (and all federal troops), Winder assumed this lesser position much to his credit and honor.

No merchant house flags were flying from the Federal Hill Telegraph Observatory, nor had there been in the present crises. The keeper, Captain Daniel Schwartzaur of the Twenty-Seventh Regiment of the Maryland Militia was then with his company on Hampstead Hill. Previously, under his supervision a 6-pound field gun had been mounted on Federal Hill for sounding the alarm at the approach of enemy vessels.[9]

Sailing Master Leonard Hall of the U. S. Sloop of War *Ontario* now took command of the hill. A correspondent of the *Baltimore Patriot* who had befriended the young officer described him as:

. . . a native of New Hampshire, [who] had endured from boyhood, in almost every clime, the hardships of a sailor's life. Having been master of a ship from the age of 17, he had embraced a wide field of observation and had acquired a species of information, calculated in times like the present, to render him valuable . . .[10]

Earlier in the war, Mr. Hall had been first officer aboard the 5-gun privateer schooner *Highflyer* of Baltimore, commanded by

Captain John Gavet in 1812.[11] In January 1813, Hall secured the command of the privateer *Wasp*, though because of the blockade he was forced to return to Baltimore.[12] On September 7, 1813, he was appointed a warrant officer in the U. S. Navy and ordered to the *Ontario*.[13]

On Federal Hill, fortifications were just beginning to be constructed. One citizen observed that the hill "ought to have been one of the earliest objects against veteran troops."[14] The view offered a splendid panorama of the city and surrounding harbor. In May 1788, the citizens had gathered there to celebrate Maryland's adoption of the Federal Constitution. Captain Joshua Barney provided a dramatic event for that occasion by having a small vessel built, completely rigged and manned, named the *Federalist*. Mounted on wheels and horse drawn through the streets, it was taken to Federal Hill amidst a large celebration.[15] And now, twenty-six years later, his new command of sailors were manning the harbor batteries.

The arrival of Commodore John Rodgers's naval command on the evening of August 25, followed by Porter's the next day, did much to calm the citizens' fears and illusions that the British army was not far below on the Washington Road. An addition to Rodgers's command was Lieutenant Solomon Rutter's command of two hundred and fifty flotillamen at the Lazaretto.[16] With the arrival of the U. S. naval forces, the Quarter-Master General of Baltimore, Paul Bentalou, requisitioned the following supplies:

> . . . I have already supplied the regiment of Militia Artillery with 99 draft horses. To the company of Marine Artillery, 24 horses for the four 18-pounders, and for Commodore Rodgers, four 12-pounders, 16 horses, with their competent number of conductors, drivers, ammunition, and baggage wagons . . .[17]

The U. S. Naval Agent in Baltimore, James Beatty, also procured tents, knapsacks, canteens, muskets, camp kettles, shoes, and blankets for Rodgers's naval brigade.[18] On the evening of the twenty-seventh, the one hundred twenty U. S. marines who had fought alongside Barney at Bladensburg, arrived in Baltimore under the corps quarter-master, Captain Samuel Bacon. The position was one that Bacon did not hold lightly. Later, in a letter of resignation, he described his duties as

. . . a tailor, blacksmith, painter, glazier, armorer, carpenter, waggoner, and butcher. Of these elevated professions I have not the happiness to be master.

Bacon referred to himself as "acting wagoner to Commodore Barney."[19]

On the morning of the twenty-eighth, Captain Alfred Grayson, the senior U. S. Marine officer in Baltimore, informed the marine commandant in Washington that his men:

. . . are much fatigued & quite destitute of clothing, tho' in fine spirits & anxious to [be] meeting the enemy again, which it is expected they will have an opportunity of doing. I have this morning tendered their services with my own to Com. Rodgers & he accepted them. In all there will be about 170 Marines. The whole force, sailors & Marines, will be tonight one thousand. The enemy is expected every hour . . .[20]

The remainder of Barney's flotillamen under Sailing Master John Webster also arrived in the city after nearly five exhaustive days since the destruction of their barges on the Patuxent.[21] Commodore Rodgers immediately combined his own command with those in Baltimore and issued his "General Orders":

The pressure of the times calling for the cooperation of the Naval Forces of our Country with those of the Army; I have by authority of Instructions from the Hon. The Sect'y of the Navy, assumed command of the Naval Forces on this Station; and to render the same as useful as possible in the present crises; do hereby direct, that a Brigade be formed of the whole, and divided into Two Regiments or Divisions. The 1st of which is to consist of the Officers, Seamen, and Marines of the U. States Frigate *Guerriere*, as well as those of the late U. States Frigate *Essex*. And the 2nd Division, of the Officers and Seamen of the Flotilla with the addition of such volunteers as may tender their services to either of said Divisions.

The 1st Regiment is to be commanded by Capt. Porter and the 2nd by Capt. Perry. Master Comd't Spence to do the duties of Adjutant. Purser Hambleton the duties of the Commissary, and Purser's Halsey and Skinner the duties of Assistant Commissaries.

Baltimore, Aug 28, 1814[22]

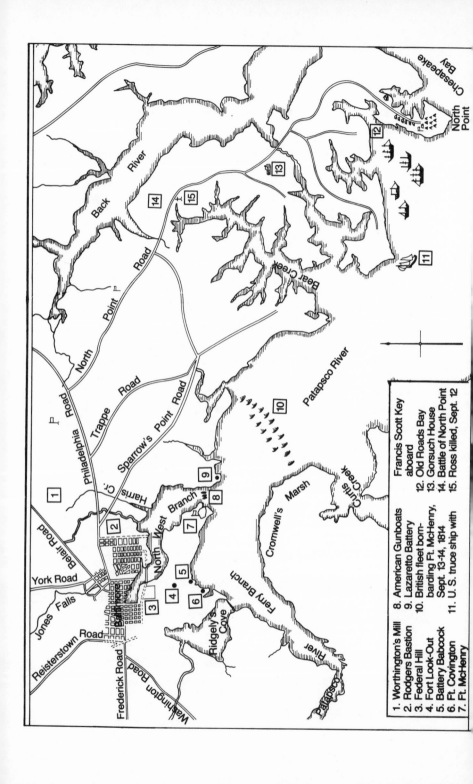

1. Worthington's Mill
2. Rodgers Bastion
3. Federal Hill
4. Fort Look-Out
5. Battery Babcock
6. Ft. Covington
7. Ft. McHenry
8. American Gunboats
9. Lazaretto Battery
10. British fleet bombarding Ft. McHenry, Sept. 13-14, 1814
11. U. S. truce ship with Francis Scott Key aboard
12. Old Roads Bay
13. Gorsuch House
14. Battle of North Point
15. Ross killed, Sept. 12

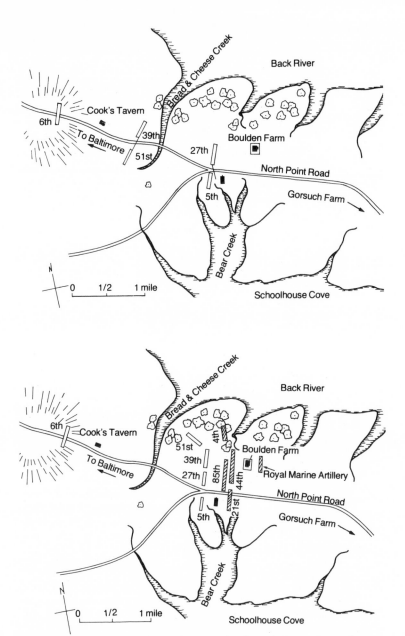

Opposite: Battle of Baltimore. *Above:* Battle of North Point, September 12, 1814. *Top:* the American defense position at 9 A.M. *Bottom:* the American position at 2:50 P.M. All three maps have been based on "Sketch of the Military Topography of Baltimore and Its Vicinity . . ." Made by order of Brigadier General Winder in 1814. National Archives, RG 77.

Purser Samuel Hambleton, a native Marylander and trusted friend of Commodore Perry, was assigned to the USS *Java* for the distribution of prize money to those officers and seamen who had served on Lake Erie a year before.[23] Many of the men, who served under Perry's blue woolen naval banner (which Hambleton helped sew) with its words *Don't Give Up The Ship*, followed the lucky Perry to Baltimore to join him on the *Java*. (This naval slogan, destined to become the navy watchword, was the last command given by the mortally wounded Captain James Lawrence, three months earlier, aboard the U. S. Frigate *Chesapeake*, in her encounter with HMS *Shannon*.)

No sooner had the city of Washington recovered from its fiery ordeal, than Captain Alexander Gordon's British flotilla sailed up the Potomac River, threatening the capital. A British officer wrote of the naval proceedings:

> . . . the ships were constantly working a distance of 50 miles in order to act against the enemy through a navigation so shallow and intricate that in spite of every exertion in buoying the channel the ships were each not less than 20 different times grounded.
>
> Fort Washington and the batteries adjacent were deserted by the garrison [under Captain Samuel Dyson] upon bursting of the first shell from the bombs after exploding their powder magazine [at 8:30 P.M. on August 27] and the whole of the twenty-seven guns which they contained & their carriages were effectually destroyed by our forces . . .[24]

On the twenty-ninth, Captain John Creighton, U. S. Navy, rode into Baltimore with a letter from the navy secretary for Rodgers. Rodgers was informed that the city of Alexandria had capitulated that morning and would, no doubt, because of its bountiful public stores, delay the British a few days in their removal. The secretary proposed the possibility of mounting guns below Alexandria to "annoy or destroy" the enemy on his return passage down the river.[25] At 10 P.M., Rodgers replied that he had detached Porter with

> . . . 100 Seamen and Marines under orders to march to Washington, but more with a view to guard the Executive, than anything else . . . I will be ready to march with all my strength at a

moment . . . for believe me, I would cheerfully spill the last of my Blood to revenge my injured country . . .[26]

Shortly after, Rodgers received orders to "repair to Bladensburg with 650 picked men."[27] Porter arrived on the thirtieth, accompanied by a detachment of marines under Captain Alfred Grayson and the remnants of the old *Essex*'s crew.[28]

The departure of Rodgers, Porter, and Perry caused General Smith great concern for Baltimore's safety. The naval force under Rodgers included the *Guerriere*'s crew and a detachment of the flotilla under Lieutenant Rutter, a total force of six hundred officers, seamen, and marines. Perry's command included a few seamen from the *Java* under Lieutenant George C. Read, and Lieutenant Colonel William Steuart's Thirty-Eighth U. S. Infantry.[29]

General Smith lost no time in writing to Rodgers to return to Baltimore immediately, for "the injury done cannot be remedied, indeed I doubt whether it can be repaired."[30] To Acting Secretary of War James Monroe, Smith wrote:

> . . . Their departure will damp the ardor of the troops & create an excitement more easily to conceive then describe. The absence of Commodore Rodgers's men has stopped the preparations for a defense for that point we are most exposed.[31]

Smith's political and military experience began to pay off. He prevented the 18-pound field guns (manned by Captain Stiles's Corps) from being carried off with Rodgers, who was acting under wishes from the War Department. These guns were the property of the War Department; however, the carriages on which they were mounted belonged to the city. At the last moment, the Committee of Vigilance and Safety upheld Smith's decision to withhold these guns believed so important for Baltimore's defense.[32]

Meanwhile, word had reached Washington that General Ross had reembarked his troops at Benedict, and with the British fleet, was now believed to be headed for Baltimore. Rodgers immediately sent word on September 1 to Lieutenant Thomas Gamble, who commanded the naval detachment sent to Washington, to return at once. Gamble, in "consequence of the fatigue of the horses" had halted on the Washington Road, three miles from Bladensburg. With the exception of one hundred men, the remainder of the *Guerriere*'s crew and the flotillamen reversed their line of march and returned to Baltimore.[33]

As materials were being assembled in Washington for Rodgers to engage Gordon's flotilla on the Potomac, the British were already busy on the wharves of Alexandria. The editor of Virginia's *Winchester Gazette*, now a citizen-soldier, witnessed the scene before him:

> The merchants stand by, viewing with melancholy countenance the British sailors gutting their warehouses of their contents. Dejection was depicted in the countenances of all I met. The enemy were busily employed in removing the tobacco and flour from the warehouses to the ships, [as] they were evidently in considerable fear of an attack, which I trust will be made upon them before two days more elapse. The gentlemen at Alexandria informed me that the conduct of the officers and sailors was respected in every sense of the word. An expedition under the command of Commodore Rodgers, Porter and Perry, is on foot to intercept their passage down the river. I met Porter and his sailors (about 120) going down last evening [August 31]. Rodgers men (about 600) will be here some time today. We are in high hopes here of success. The object will be to attack them, as they descend the river from both sides. Embankments are throwing up for the heavy cannon . . . Tonight will perhaps be an important one.[34]

Captain Gordon's flotilla remained in Alexandria for three days before receiving orders to rejoin the fleet. On September 2, Rodgers's own flotilla proceeded from Washington with

> three small fire vessels under the protection of 4 Barges or Cutters, manned with about sixty seamen armed with muskets, destined against two of the enemy's frigates and a bomb ship, which layed about 2½ miles below Alexandria.

Rodgers's principal officers on this expedition included Lieutenants Henry Newcomb and Delaney Forrest, Sailing Master James Ramage, and Master's Mate Robert Stockton, all from the *Guerriere*.[35]

For the next three days, Gordon's return passage down the Potomac was harassed day and night by Porter's battery at Indian Head, Maryland; by Perry's battery at White House, a bluff ten miles below Mount Vernon, Virginia; and by Rodgers's flotilla, who annoyed the enemy from behind. In Baltimore, a lady wrote, "There was a great cannonading heard here yesterday, supposed to be 30 or 40 miles distant."[36]

By the evening of the fifth, Gordon had successfully removed his flotilla and twenty-one prize merchant vessels from the Potomac, having run the gauntlet of American shore batteries. Rodgers and Perry were ordered to return to Baltimore as the enemy was "in a situation to make a rapid move on Baltimore."[37] Rodgers reported to the navy department his assessment of the Potomac encounter.

Although I did not succeed in the destruction of any of the enemy's vessels, I am nevertheless convinced that the expedition was in many points of view attended with good effect . . .[38]

On the evening of the sixth, a correspondent for the *National Intelligencer* viewed their departure from Washington:

Fourteen wagons—full of our noble seamen, the first surmounted with the well-known standard of Free Trade and Sailor's Rights, the whole proceeded by the Hero of Valparaiso and cheered by their boatswain's whistle, passed through this city on their way to Baltimore Tuesday evening.[39]

Rodgers's earlier departure from Baltimore on August 30 prompted a disagreement over the authority of command between the officers of the flotilla and that of Captain Robert Spence, whom Rodgers had left in command during his absence.[40] Lieutenant Solomon Frazier (left in command of the flotilla at Baltimore) had refused to obey and act under Spence's command.[41] General Smith, not wanting to interfere with internal naval affairs, requested by letter to Rodgers that he ask the naval secretary to intercede with a directive order.[42]

Aware of the discrete nature of the Chesapeake Flotilla in relation to that of the regular navy, Jones wrote to Captain Spence that Frazier's refusal had resulted "from a mistaken sense of duty . . . and not from a spirit of insubordination."[43] Jones reiterated the need in the present crisis for "harmony and mutual existance" between the two naval units.[44]

When word reached the recuperating flotilla commander at his home, Joshua Barney immediately sent a private letter to the navy secretary defending his officers:

. . . Captain Spence is not a character to meet the approbation of the officers and men lately under my command. His open hostility to the flotilla in the spring, his conduct and that of his fellow officers at the time of the transfer of the *Ontario* men, his avowed opposition to the Administration, his unsocial manners . . . his refusal to proceed to Sackets Harbor, his youth and inexperiences has rendered him obnoxious to all. My officers have complained of all this to me, but, they all declare that if Com. Rodgers, Perry or Porter was but at their head they would be contented . . .[45]

Despite the differences of opinion between Captain Spence and the flotilla officers, Jones was not about to have a scandal develop within his department with Baltimore in peril. The regulations were quite clear. Rodgers would soon return and the matter would be cleared up.

Upon returning to Baltimore, Rodgers and Perry were quartered at the Old Fountain Inn, establishing their field headquarters upon Hampstead Hill.[46] Captain David Porter was ordered to New York harbor to take command of Robert Fulton's new steam battery, the *Demologos*, near completion there.[47]

From Hampstead Hill, Rodgers could easily look down the Patapsco River, past the ramparts of Fort McHenry to the Chesapeake Bay nearly twelve miles away. Rodgers outfitted his naval line, known as Rodgers Bastion, with an array of naval and field artillery amounting to sixteen guns. Rodgers had acquired fourteen 12-pounders on traveling carriages and two long 12-pounders on naval carriages from the U. S. Sloop of War *Erie*.[48]

Beginning near the mouth of Harris Creek near Fell's Point, the earthen gun batteries and entrenchments continued over Hampstead Hill to the Philadelphia Road. The northernmost line extended from there to the Belair Road, and was manned by the First Regiment of Maryland Artillery. The regiment consisted of seven companies, each having an artillery equipage of 4-pounder and 6-pounder field guns.[49]

To the rear of the militia batteries, Brigadier General Tobias Stansbury, commanding the Eleventh Brigade, and Brigadier General Thomas Foreman, commanding the First Brigade, established their militia infantry units. Commanding the city's own elite Third Brigade, which included the First Regiment of Artillery, was Brigadier General John Stricker.[50] Captain George Stiles's Corps of Seamen manned five 18-pound field guns in support of the lines.

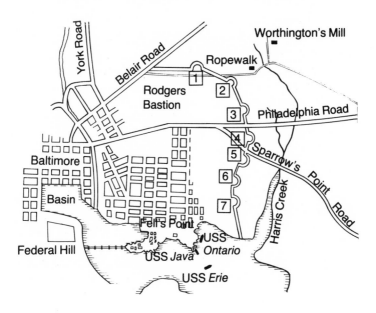

Rodgers Bastion, September 12-14, 1814. The distribution of the "naval" shore batteries on the heights of Hampstead Hill. The entrenchments between the batteries were occupied by the U. S. Marines and companies of the Maryland and Pennsylvania militia.

Key: 1-2. First Regiment of Artillery, Maryland Volunteer Militia; 3. Captain Stiles' Marine Artillery; 4. Lt. Gamble; 5. Sailing Master Roche & Midshipman Field; 6. Sailing Master Ramage; 7. Midshipman Salter. Based on "Sketch of the Military Topography of Baltimore and Its Vicinity . . ."

The citizens who dug the entrenchments and naval gun batteries witnessed the preparations of the sailors as they were exercised "into the use of the musket, as practiced by the land forces." For those that beheld them, these land maneuvers provided an awkward scene. It was described in the *Niles' Weekly Register*

AMERICAN SEAMEN

. . . The crew of the ship [*Guerriere*], some days before the attack, were armed with muskets and paraded, in squads or companies of 60 or 70 men each, for drill. Their officers were zealous and attentive, and certainly had need of all their patience to bear with, (as it appeared to me,) the studied awkwardness of the sailors—who, evidently, did not like such maneuvering. After one of the squads, with great labor, had been placed in line, the officer began with "attention;"—and *"silence"*—*"hold your jaw,"* said at least every other man of them. "Silence," cried the officer, vexed—and *"aye, aye, sir,"* or *"silence,"* said the whole!

Order being obtained, the gentleman commanding, with the greatest patience and perspicuity, described to them what he wished them to do, encouraging them to do it handsomely. They seemed exceedingly anxious to hear the "speech," as I heard one of them call it; and by the time he had finished his directions, they got themselves into the shape of a half moon, the wings drawing up to him a little and little, without his noticing it at the moment. He peremptorily ordered them back, and back they went as fast as they could; when they began telling each other what the officer meant, chattering at a mighty rate. Silence being had, "Jack" prepared himself to do as well as he could, but went here, there, and everywhere, lost in glorious confusion. The commander frequently turned his head aside to conceal a smile, but the spectators laughed most heartily, to the great pleasure of the sailors, who loved to make fun. Things went this way for about an hour, and everybody was puzzled to find out whether the sailors were really so awkward as they appeared, or not. But at last the manner of "charging bayonet" was told to them, and they were informed that to "charge" and "to board" was the same thing. Here they were *at home*—their eyes glistened, every fellow gathered up his sinews to their utmost strength, and waited with profound silence for the word. It was given—and on they came with fearful impetuosity, everyone striving to get foremost;—it happened that a horse and cart was in their way—several of the spectators had retreated behind it; but the sailors came jumping over it like squirrels, and dashing among them, made them fly off at full speed, to the great delight of the seamen and amidst peals of laughter from all that were looking on. Never, perhaps, since time began, was there a more efficient body of men than this crew, as seamen—nor did it appear possible (we speak from the knowledge of persons on whose judgement we entirely depend) that, as sailors, they could be better drilled to *the business of a ship*, but as *soldiers*, except in a courage that knew no fear, and a zeal that anticipated no check, they were the *querrest* and most odd set of fellows that ever were collected together. *They were as a host to Baltimore.*[51]

Indeed, the naval entrenchments upon Hampstead Hill had taken on the appearance of a fully armed frigate, with guns run out through embrasures and with sailors armed with muskets, cutlasses, and boarding pikes. The one hundred seventy U. S. marines were situated to the rear to support the naval batteries.

On Saturday morning, September 10, General Winder visited Fort Covington garrisoned by Captain William Addison's U. S. Sea Fencibles. In a communique to Smith, Winder reported that ". . . out of 93 men . . . one half are unfit for duty from the unhealthiness of the situation and the number of sick is daily increasing . . ."[52]

The unhealthiness of the garrison was due to the bilious fever which had plagued the fort since 1813. This placed Fort McHenry's western approaches nearly unprotected. General Smith consequently conferred with Rodgers to send a naval detachment to man the fort as well as the six-gun Battery Babcock.

While intelligence reports continued to come in, Vice Admiral Cochrane collected his scattered naval forces near Tangier Island in the bay, and sailed towards Baltimore. To Lieutenant Solomon Rutter at the Lazaretto, Rodgers offered a note to prepare the flotillamen:

There were twelve sail of the enemy in sight of Annapolis this evening; also some small craft in advance standing up the bay with a fresh breeze. I give you this information, that you may issue the necessary orders to the Flotilla to prevent surprize.[53]

As Baltimore prepared for invasion, events in Washington and Upper Marlboro concerning the British arrest of an esteemed American citizen were being discussed. These inquiries to high British and American officials by friends who were concerned eventually led to the circumstances surrounding the writing of a poem, later to be entitled *The Star-Spangled Banner.*

7 ☆ ☆ ☆ ☆ ☆ ☆ ☆

A FLAG OF TRUCE

Francis Scott Key, a thirty-five-year-old volunteer militia aide, was in the midst of the American retreat as he rode westward on Pennsylvania Avenue, past the President's House, toward Georgetown. A night of extreme confusion and despair filled Washington as the remnants of Winder's army streamed by.

A native Marylander, Key was educated at St. John's College in Annapolis and began law practice in 1801 in his hometown of Frederick, Maryland.[1] Soon thereafter, he moved with his family to Georgetown, Maryland, where he hoped to establish a lucrative practice. He was a devout member of the Episcopal Church and author of numerous poems and hymns. He was also conscious of his country's peril. In June 1814, he joined Major George Peters's militia company of the Georgetown Field Artillery as a lieutenant-quartermaster and served briefly on the Patuxent.[2]

In late August, when the British were marching towards Washington, Key volunteered as an aide to General Walter Smith, commanding the First Brigade of the District militia. His duty was to delegate positions for the various companies as they arrived on the field of Bladensburg.[3] However, later, when the Americans were forced to abandon their final defensive position, Key followed the retreating army, as the British pressed slowly forward, and entered the nation's capital. Later that evening, Key and his family witnessed the fiery occupation of Washington from their Bridge Street residence in Georgetown.

In Baltimore the newspapers were filled with reports of events in Washington, and the local citizens followed these accounts with great interest. One such account is of special relevance to the story of Francis Scott Key and the birth of the National Anthem. The August 30 edition of the *Baltimore Federal Gazette* published the details concerning the arrest of Dr. William Beanes, the once amiable host to Major General Robert Ross.

> . . . after the enemy had passed Marlborough, Robert Bowie, Esq., formerly governor of this state, came into the town and proposed to make prisoners of some of the [British] stragglers who were following the main body on their retreat; this proposition was asserted by Doctor Beanes who resided in the town; and although several gentlemen who were present urged the dangerous consequences that might result from it while the enemy were so near, they proceeded to put their plan into execution, and actually took six prisoners which they sent to Queen Anne about 9 miles distant.[4]

The self-appointed citizens' committee might have succeeded had it not been for the escape of one of the British soldiers who immediately informed General Ross. As the *Gazette* explained:

> The consequence of this officious proceeding proved very unpleasant. About one o'clock next morning a party of British horsemen arrived in the town, took Doctor Beanes and two other gentlemen who were in bed in his house, mounted them on horses without saddles and conveyed them as prisoners to the British camp . . .[5]

Upon the negotiated release of the British soldiers, General Ross let the Americans go—except for Doctor Beanes. Ross considered the doctor's involvement in this affair as a breach of faith, considering the doctor's earlier stance in regard to the war. Beanes was removed to the British fleet at Benedict and sequestered aboard the British flagship, HMS *Tonnant*.

Immediately his friends began the arduous task of obtaining his release. Despite several initial inquiries, no progress was made. On September 1, a friend of Beanes's, Richard West, decided, on behalf of the doctor, to obtain the services of a mutual friend. He visited

Francis Scott Key who listened to the details concerning the ordeal of
their mutual friend.

Key accepted the challenge to assist and began to assert his
influence on the president to obtain official government sanction to
visit the British fleet. Receiving letters of instruction and introduc-
tion, Key went on to Baltimore to acquire the services of Colonel
John S. Skinner, the United States Agent for Prisoner Exchange.[6]
Skinner, a twenty-six-year-old Baltimorean, was also Washington's
agent for official dispatches to the British high command.

Key carried personal letters from British officers who had been
wounded at Bladensburg, who wrote in praise of the medical treat-
ment offered by the Americans, among them Dr. Beanes. Before
leaving for Baltimore on September 3, Key addressed a letter to his
mother:

> . . . I am going in the morning to Balt. to proceed in a flag-vessel
> to Gen'l Ross. Old Dr. Beanes of Marlboro is taken prisoner by
> the enemy, who threaten to carry him off. Some of his friends
> have urged me to apply for a flag [of truce] & go & try to procure
> his release. I hope to return in about 8 or 10 days, though it is
> uncertain, as I do not know where to find the fleet . . .[7]

Four days later on a vessel obtained under the auspices of Colonel
Skinner, Key and Skinner encountered the British fleet on the Chesapeake. They were taken on board Vice Admiral Cochrane's flagship,
HMS *Tonnant*, and following a dinner with Ross and Cockburn
secured the release of Dr. Beanes.

However, the British were preparing for an attack against Baltimore and for security reasons decided to detain the Americans. Staff
officers had come aboard and all available berths were needed. The
Americans were transferred to the care of Captain Thomas Cochrane
(the Admiral's son) on board HMS *Surprize*, with the truce vessel in
tow.[8]

On September 9, the British fleet met with Captain Gordon's
flotilla in the Potomac, and then returned to the Chesapeake. At
dawn, on the tenth, Vice Admiral Cochrane's expeditionary fleet,
consisting of some fifty warships, made sail for Baltimore. Key,
Skinner, and Beanes were transferred back to their own vessel on
the eleventh, and from that vantage point, were forced to witness
with apprehension the conclusion of the British campaign against
Baltimore.[9]

8 ☆ ☆ ☆ ☆ ☆ ☆ ☆

FOUR DAYS IN SEPTEMBER

SUNDAY, SEPTEMBER 11

At 10 A.M., Commodore John Rodgers, having met with Major George Armistead at Fort McHenry, sent a communique to General Smith:

> Sir, I have just ordered an officer & 80 sailors to occupy Fort Wadsworth [Covington], the sea fencibles now there being all sick. The Six Gun Battery . . . I shall have manned if possible by a detachment from the flotilla. I am now making my distribution . . .[1]

Later in his official report to the naval secretary, Rodgers employed his command as follows:

> . . . In the general distribution of the forces employed in the defense of Baltimore, with the concurrance of the commanding General, I stationed Lt. Gamble, first of the *Guerriere*, with about 100 seamen, in command of a Seven Gun Battery, on the line between the Roads leading from Phila. and Sparrow's Point.
>
> Sailing Master De La Roche of the *Erie*, and Midsh. Field of the *Guerriere*, with 20 seamen, in command of a Two Gun Battery fronting the Road leading from Sparrow's Point.
>
> Sailing Master Ramage, of the *Guerriere*, with 80 seamen, in command of a Five Gun Battery, to the right of the Sparrow's Point Road.
>
> And Midsh. Salter, with 12 seamen, in command of a One Gun Battery a little to the right of Mr. Ramage.

Lt. Kuhn with the Detachment of Marines belonging to the *Guerriere* was posted in the entrenchment between the Batteries occupied [by] Lt. Gamble and Sailing Master Ramage.

Lt. Newcomb, third of the *Guerriere,* with 80 seamen occupied Fort Covington, on the Ferry Branch, a little below Spring Gardens.

Sailing Master Webster, of the Flotilla with 50 seamen of that corps occupied a Six Gun Battery on the Ferry Branch, known by the name of Fort Babcock. Lt. Frazier of the Flotilla, with 45 seamen of the same corps, occupied a Three Gun Battery near the Lazaretto. And Lt. Rutter, the Senior Officer of the Flotilla in command of all the Barges, which were moored at the entrance of the Passage between the Lazaretto and Fort McHenry, in the left Wing of the Water Battery, at which was stationed S. Master Rodman and 60 seamen of the Flotilla . . .[2]

The flotillamen sent to Fort McHenry filled the vacancy previously left by Captain Stiles's Corps of Seamen. Detachments of seamen were placed in the city barges and at the Lazaretto, establishing formidable naval shore and floating batteries to defend the harbor entrance. Lieutenant Rutter reported to Rodgers on the defense preparations:

Sir, I hereby report to you the Battery with three long eighteen pounders at the Lazaretto is fit for service, with one hundred rounds [of ammunition] and manned agreeable to your orders. Eight Barges [are] up with long eights and four with long Twelves and all with gunades. Eighteens manned and ready for service. Three small barges [and] the three Large Barges are at the Point, yet under the Direction of the Navy Agent.

Men Distributed as Follows

8 Barges, each 34 men	272
3 Small Barges, each 22 men	66
Men on board *Erie*	24
In the Battery	45
Remaining at the Lazaretto	114
Total	521
Deserted, unfit for service & sick	⁻50
	471

Lazaretto, September 11, 1814
Sol. Rutter
Lieut. U. S. Flotilla[3]

At noon, as the British fleet appeared off North Point, the alarm gun on Federal Hill sounded the enemy's approach. The nine London-cast bells in the belfry of Reverend James Kemp's Christ's Church joined in sounding the alarm.[4]

Soon, militia soldiers rushed to join their respective companies at Pratt and Light streets.[5] At 3 P.M., Brigadier John Stricker's well-trained Third Brigade, a total of some 3,185 men, marched out of the city.[6] On the steps of his residence, the Reverend John Glendy blessed the soldiers and prayed for their safety and success. En route, amidst the cheers of the citizenry, they passed through the ranks of the U. S. marines and Lieutenant Gamble's naval battery.

With regimental flags flying, marching to the martial beat of fifes and drums, the Americans set forth upon the North Point Road. By early evening they had marched the seven miles down to the Old Methodist Meeting House, to a planned line of defense, and encamped for the night.

Bombardment of Fort McHenry, circa 1814, artist unknown. Courtesy of The Peale Museum, Baltimore, Maryland.

Commodore John Rodgers informed General Smith from the Lazaretto that evening that

> . . . the enemy were still at anchor between North Point and Sparrow's Point . . . Should it be calm tomorrow morning . . . it would be to our advantage to sink seven or 8 vessels as obstructions . . .[7]

For Commodore Oliver Hazard Perry writing to a friend:

> It is, at this moment, said the enemy are now standing up the river for this place with about 40 sail. I shall stay by my ship and take no part in the militia fight. I expect to have to burn her.[8]

MONDAY, SEPTEMBER 12

On the morning of September 12, Musician Henry Lightner looked down the broad expanse of the Patapsco River. A drummer in Captain John Berry's Washington Artillerists, he was stationed behind the parapets of Fort McHenry's water batteries. The company was one of three detachments from the First Regiment of the Maryland Militia Artillery, Third Brigade, that were ordered to the fort. The others were the Baltimore Independent Artillerists, commanded by Lieutenant Charles Pennington, and Captain Joseph Nicholson's U. S. volunteer company of the Baltimore Fencibles.[9]

In addition, detachments of the U. S. infantry were ordered to the fort under the command of Lieutenant Colonel William Steuart (the Thirty-Eighth) and Major Samuel Lane (the Fourteenth). These consisted of an incomplete company of the Twelfth under Captain Thomas Sangsten; two companies of the Thirty-Sixth under Captain Joseph Hook and Lieutenant William L. Rogers; and four companies of the Thirty-Eighth, commanded by Captains Samuel C. Leakin, Charles Stansbury, Joseph H. Hook, and John Buck, a total of an estimated six hundred officers and enlisted men.[10]

Quartered within the fort was Major Armistead's company of regulars, the U. S. Corps of Artillery, commanded by Captain Frederick Evans.[11] On August 26, in a letter to the adjutant general in Philadelphia, Evans wrote:

> . . . We are here all hurry and confusion. I have at this moment the command of 60 men making musket cartridges, and the casting of ball. Also I must prepare four twelves with their am-

munition complete for Com. Rodgers men. You will readily see my situation as [Major] Armistead is out on important business and we expect an attack tomorrow or the next day . . .[12]

Since Saturday evening, the tenth, the British naval fleet had been sighted, gathering off North Point. As the light of day improved visibility, Major Armistead could distinguish the sails of larger vessels—frigates and ships of the line. But more alarming was the sight of bomb ships and numerous landing launches. The British had landed at North Point.

Musician Lightner began to beat the alarm on his drum. Militia Private Gilbert Cassard, a French refugee who had escaped the slave revolt in Santo Domingo several years before, stood stoically by his gun to defend his adopted country.[13] Behind the ramparts of Fort McHenry's southwest bastion, Isaac Munroe, a private in the Baltimore Fencibles waited by his gun battery. Lieutenant Levi Claggett, a prosperous flour merchant and investor in Baltimore's privateer trade, was in charge of the 24-pounders. Mr. Munroe knew the importance of the moment and what had occurred the past few days, as he was one of the editors of the *Baltimore Patriot*, a daily city paper. Munroe later described the situation at Fort McHenry prior to the battle, in a letter dated September 17, to a friend in Boston:

. . . I will give you an account of the approach of the enemy before this place, so far as it came under my observation. On Saturday last and the day previous, we had intelligence that the enemy had collected all his force, to the amount of 47 sail, and were proceeding down the bay, consequently we were led to hope we should have a little rest from our incessant labors, in preparing to resist them. On Saturday noon, Major Armistead, the commander of Fort McHenry, permitted Chief Justice Nicholson who commands a volunteer corps of 80 men, to march to town, holding ourselves in readiness to return the instant he thought prudent to call. As it turned out, while we were marching to town, the enemy tacked about and just at dusk, were seen under a press of sail, with a fair wind, approaching the town. Their movements were closely watched at the Fort, and at half past 9 o'clock [P.M.] Judge Nicholson received orders to repair to the Fort before 12 [midnight], although the rain poured down in torrents.

On our arrival we found the matches burning, the [hot shot] furnaces heated and vomiting red shot, and everything ready for a gallant defense . . .[14]

The alarm spread throughout the countryside. The Battle of Baltimore had begun. The British land forces had landed at North Point with no American resistance. Lieutenant George Gleig of the 85th Light Infantry described the landing:

. . . The moon had set, and there was no light in the sky, except that which a multitude of brilliant stars afforded, when a general stir throughout the fleet gave notice that the moment of disembarkation was at hand. The soldiers, rousing from their sleep, began to assemble upon the decks in the order in which it had been previously agreed that they should step into the boats; the seamen, applying sedulously to their tasks, hoisted out barges, launches, gigs, &c., with all dispatch; whilst the few stores deemed essential to the operations of the campaign were so arranged, as to be transported at once from the shipping to the beach. All, however, was done in profound silence . . . All this took place before the first blush of dawn had shown itself on the eastern horizon. Nor was the remainder of the army tardy in reaching its destination.

Exerting themselves to the utmost, our gallant tars, without any intermission of labour for several hours, pulled backwards and forwards, and by seven o'clock, infantry, artillery, baggage, and horses, appeared to be all on shore . . . I should be disposed to say, that somewhere about five thousand, or five thousand five hundred men, moved from the water's edge this morning . . .[15]

Sailing Master George De La Roche watched from the deck of the U. S. Sloop of War *Erie* anchored off Fort McHenry. Her 32-pound carronades were primed and ready. A portion of her twenty-four-man crew of officers and seamen had been borrowed from the flotilla as she was undermanned.[16]

Roche previously had served aboard the U. S. Frigate *Constellation* in June of 1813 as Acting Sailing Master of Gunboat *No. 74* anchored near Craney Island, Virginia. On June 22, 1813, he helped prevent a British offensive to capture the island as well as the *Constellation*. He was subsequently promoted to his present position and on August 1, was ordered to the *Erie*.[17]

On September 12, 1814, Roche recorded in his diary:

. . . having at daylight discovered that the British had succeeded in forcing three frigates inside the Man of War Shoals 15 miles below, and were coming up with a fine breeze, contrary to our expectations. I sent word to Commo. J. Rodgers then in command, and as our own broadside was too light to withstand frigates, was ordered to bring the ship near Baltre. again. Began to sink ships in the channel, and then was given by Commo. Rodgers the command of the most advanced battery between the Philadelphia & Sparrow's Point Road, three hundred yards in advance of all others, of three 12 pounders, thirty two officers & men, and military corps for small arms . . .[18]

The twenty-three-year-old sailing master was described by Captain Spence as "an active sailor, and a gentlemanly officer, whose diligent exertions, and assistance to me while making preparations for the defense of this city, were conspicious."[19] The *Erie* now lay in the basin, off Jackson's Wharf near Fell's Point "with springs on her cables to prevent the foe from coming up to the city in boats."[20]

On board the *Erie* a young Baltimorean, Midshipman George Nicholas Hollins, five days shy of his fifteenth birthday, was about to be exposed to a baptism of fire. He had received a warrant officer's position earlier in February upon being introduced to Commodore Perry, a guest in his father's house. At this moment, young Hollins stood firmly as acting commanding officer upon the gun deck and awaited the British advance.[21]

The shore defenses on the Ferry Branch of the Patapsco River to the west of Fort McHenry provided quite a formidable series of shore gun batteries. At Fort Covington, Lieutenant Henry Newcomb was busily preparing the French 18-pounders under his command. Encamped to the rear of the fort was the Fifty-Sixth Regiment of Virginia Infantry Militia, a total of 561 men, under the command of Lieutenant Colonel Griffin Taylor.[22]

A few hundred yards to the east of Covington, Sailing Master John Webster commanded the six-gun Battery Babcock mounted with six French 18-pound naval guns. Webster described his battery as

opened and exposed, except a breastwork of dirt thrown up about four feet high, with a magazine in the rear about sixty feet off, composed of a hole dug in the side of a hill as security for the ammunition.[23]

Commanding seventy-five flotillamen, he lent twenty-three of these to Lieutenant George Budd, commander of Fort Look-Out (also known as Fort Wood), a few hundred feet to the rear, upon a high hilltop.[24] Lieutenant Budd instructed his own men in the filling of 120 flannel cartridge bags with powder capable of discharging shot from one of his seven 24-pound naval guns taken off the frigate *Java*.[25]

Captain Samuel Babcock, of the U. S. Corps of Engineers, formulated a plan to cut down pine trees to construct a palisade around the circular-shaped battery.[26]

Earlier that morning, while Baltimore prepared its defenses, Major General Robert Ross rapidly moved the British army and naval detachments up the North Point Road toward the city. The Maryland countryside was admired by officer and private alike. Lieutenant Gleig, of the Eighty-Fifth Light Infantry, described the rural landscape:

> . . . Having cleared the open fields, we soon found ourselves in a country resembling, in many respects, that which we had traversed in our late operations; that is to say, thick woods hemmed us in on every side, and the spots of cultivated soil were few and of small compass. There was, however, one striking difference to be observed. Little lakes, or other large ponds, abounded here; they were equally plentiful on both sides of the way; and being in general deep enough to hinder us from fording, they, for the most part, occasioned us no little trouble, and some fatigue, before we succeeded in passing them. Small streams, likewise, landing in the heads of creeks, more than once interrupted our progress. In a word, the country presented a thousand defensible posts, even to a people so little accustomed as we were to examine a country with the eye of soldiers; and it surprized us not a little to find, that no attempt was made to defend it . . .[27]

Since dawn, Brigadier General Stricker's reconnaissance force had been waiting. It was now past noon. An hour before, Colonel James Biay's vedette had sighted General Ross's vanguard at the Gorsuch House three miles ahead, awaiting the arrival of the main British force. Stricker had positioned Captain Montgomery's Union Artillery, with six field guns, across the North Point Road, flanked by two militia infantry regiments, the Fifth and Twenty-Seventh, with the Fifty-First and Thirty-Ninth to the rear. Behind this second reserve, a half-mile to the rear, was stationed the Sixth. His strategy was to have these three defensive lines act in concert with each other; therefore, the first line, having received the primary British attack, would, if necessary, fall back through the second reserve and form on the right of the Sixth.[28]

Rather than risk a possible attack at night, Stricker decided to provoke a general engagement while his troops were still in a spirited situation to engage. Militia forces, unlike regulars, could not be trusted in a well-disciplined night defense against veteran troops, especially ones so experienced in the art of warfare.

At 1 P.M., General Stricker moved forward a volunteer vanguard comprised of 250 men of the Fifth Regiment, under the immediate command of Major Richard Health. Earlier, while Admiral Cockburn and General Ross took advantage of Maryland hospitality by break-fasting at the Gorsuch House, three American dragoons who had been captured were brought in and interrogated. Upon questioning, the Americans replied with a fair, perhaps overstated, account of Smith's militia command, but held back any information regarding Stricker's command, just up the road. Informed that Smith's command was mainly militia, Ross replied that he didn't care "if it rains militia."[29]

Assuming that only vedettes of the militia awaited ahead, General Ross set out shortly before noon with Admiral Cockburn to reconnoiter with a small advance party. Within a period of an hour, Major Health's own advance command, moving cautiously down the road, soon encountered Ross's party. In the heavily wooded area, musket fire was exchanged. "The Americans outnumbered us beyond calculation," Lieutenant Gleig related,

> whilst, as individuals, they were at least our equals in the skill with which they used their weapon; yet, from the very commencement, it was on our part a continual advance, on theirs a continual retreat.[30]

In the few brief moments following, the campaign against these upstart Baltimoreans was altered by a young private of Captain Edward Aisquith's rifle company of sharpshooters who were on the flanks of the British advance. General Ross and Admiral Cockburn became concerned that they had fallen into a serious misfortune, so far advanced of their main force, and rode ahead. Finding a larger American force than anticipated, Ross rode back to hurry up the light infantry. Lieutenant Gleig's narrative relates what transpired.

> . . . How bitterly had the whole expedition cause to lament that step! He had scarsely entered the wood, when an American rifleman singled him out; he fired, and the ball, true to its mark, pierced his side. When the General received his death-wound, I chanced to be standing at no great distance from him; I saw that he was struck, for the reins dropped instantly from his hand, and he leaned forward upon the pommel of his saddle . . . His horse making a movement forward, he lost his seat, and, but for the intervention of his aide-de-camp's arm must have fallen to the ground. As it was, we could only lay him at length upon the grass, for his limbs could no longer perform their office—it was but too manifest that his race was run . . .[31]

Ross requested that Colonel Arthur Brooke, commander of the Forty-Fourth Foot be immediately summoned. Now thrust into command of the British army, Brook was to be characterized as "an officer of decided personal courage, but, perhaps, better calculated to lead a battalion, than to guide an army."[32] Ross, while being transported back to the fleet in a wagon, died en route, having been unable to begin his determined effort to dislodge Smith from Hampstead Hill. Later, in a dispatch to London, Colonel Brooke spoke eloquently of the forty-eight-year-old Irish-born general:

> . . . Thus fell, at an early age, one of the brightest ornaments of his profession; one who, whether at the head of a regiment, a brigade, or corps, had alike displayed the talents of command; who was not less beloved in his private, than enthusiatically admired in his public character; and whose only fault, if it may be deemed so, was an excess of gallantry, enterprize, and devotion to the service . . .[33]

Major Health's command, receiving a heavy fire, pulled back to Stricker's main defense line, while the British Eighty-Fifth Foot, Light Infantry, arrived in view of Stricker's main defense lines, supported by the Congreve Rocket Batteries of the Royal Marine Artillery. Colonel Brooke ordered his field artillery and rocket batteries to open upon the American center and left flank, providing an opportunity for a British flanking movement. Stricker, foreseeing the movement, ordered forward the Thirty-Ninth and Fifty-First Maryland Militia Infantry into line on his left flank. Unable to perform what is known in military parlance as a "wheeling movement," the inexperienced Fifty-First became confused in this complicated maneuver amidst the artillery duel that had commenced between the two opposing regiments. Taking advantage of the momentary confusion, Brooke vigorously pushed forward his light infantry to turn the American left under a relentless volley of musketry.[34]

Lieutenant Gleig, stationed along in front of the opposing American center, noted the near climax of the Battle of North Point:

> . . . A hearty British cheer gave notice of our willingness to meet them, and firing and running we gradually closed upon them, with the design of bringing the bayonet into play . . . Volley upon volley having been given, we were now advanced within less than twenty yards of the American line; yet such was the denseness of the smoke, that it was only when a passing breeze swept away the cloud for a moment, that either force became visible to the other . . . The flashes of the enemy's muskets alone served as an object to aim at, as, without doubt, the flashes of our muskets alone guided the enemy . . .[35]

Unable to hold their position on the left flank, the Fifty-First wavered under the assault, then pulled hastily back taking part of the Thirty-Ninth with them. The American center and right flank held by Captain Montgomery's Union Artillery and the Fifth Maryland Regiment stood firm, inflicting heavy casualties on the British Twenty-First and Forty-Fourth regiments.[36]

Stricker, concerned that his command might be routed by the exposed left flank, ordered his force to pull back. In his official report afterwards to Major General Smith, Stricker addressed his situation:

> . . . I was constrained to order a movement back to the reserve regiment [the 6th], under Colonel McDonald, which was well posted to receive the retired line which mostly rallied well. On forming with the 6th, the fatigued state of the regiments and corps which had retired, and the probability that my right flank might be turned by a quick movement of the enemy in that direction, induced me, after proper deliberation, to fall back to Worthington's Mill; which I was the more persuaded to, by my desire to have the 6th regiment (whose officers and men were eager to share

the dangers of their brother soldiers) perfect and in good order to receive the enemy on his nearer approach to the city . . .[37]

General Stricker had held his Third Brigade as long as safely possible. His orders from General Smith had been only to delay the British advance. Stricker moved his command the four and a half miles back to Baltimore, and repositioned the Third Brigade to the left of the American defenses a half mile in front of Hampstead Hill.

Confusion temporarily swept Baltimore as word reached the city that Stricker's force was pulling back. The citizens remembered all too well what had happened at Washington, barely three weeks before.

At 4 P.M., Brigadier General Thomas Foreman, commanding the First Brigade, gave orders for the burning of the great ropewalk of Calief & Shinnick to prevent it from falling into the enemy's hands. More importantly the ropewalk, which contained the hemp and cordage for the frigate *Java*, stood nearly in front of the American lines. "The burning of this ropewalk," an observer wrote,

> created a very brilliant light, whilst it lasted, and the occasion of great alarm to many of the inhabitants of the city and surrounding country, that beheld it at a distance and knew not the cause.[38]

The thick black smoke, fed by the large quantities of naval stores, drifted southward along the American entrenchments, adding to the despair of the people.

Brigadier General Winder, commanding the western defenses, was ordered to Hampstead Hill with the Virginia Brigade and a U. S. Light Dragoon company under Captain Bird, taking a position to the left of the Third Brigade. At Fort McHenry, Major George Armistead kept a vigil on the movements of the British fleet. Within his quarters he wrote a note to General Smith:

> From the number of barges and the well known situation of the enemy, I have not a doubt but that an assault will be made this night upon the fort.[39]

As daylight began to fade, Sailing Master Leonard Hall watched from Federal Hill, as did many Baltimoreans viewing the awesome scene before them. The British naval support squadron, sixteen vessels in all, was proceeding up towards Fort McHenry. British Midshipman Robert Barrett described the naval advance from the deck of the HMS *Hebrus:*

. . . Thus departing from our gallant comrades, we proceeded, without delay, under all sail, in company with the frigates, sloops, and bombs, &c., to take up a position where we might be enabled to attack the sea defenses of Baltimore. Leaving the line-of-battle-ships, which on account of their size, could not proceed any farther than North Point, our frigates sailed through the mud for miles . . . As we proceeded up the river, doubtless the Americans were struck with panic and amazement, for although they built frigates at this port, yet they always sailed down the river, flying light, as far as Annapolis, where, I was informed, they completed for sea, by taking in their guns, provisions, and water . . .[40]

Vice Admiral Cochrane transferred his broad pennant to HMS *Surprize*, Captain Edward Codrington, Captain of the Fleet, commanding. To his wife in London, Codrington wrote:

. . . The work of destruction is now about to begin and there will probably be many broken heads tonight. The army with as many seamen and marines as possibly could be spared were all landed this morning and are now on their march to the town of Baltimore . . . The bomb vessels, brigs & frigates, are all pushing up the river with an eagerness which must annoy the enemy, I presume as much as it delights me . . .[41]

TUESDAY, SEPTEMBER 13

The fire which destroyed the ropewalk of Calief & Shinnick was extinguished by a rainstorm during the night. Captain Matthias Bartgis's Sixteenth Maryland Militia Infantry remained in a column to the rear of Rodgers Bastion. To their right were Major Randall's Pennsylvania Volunteer Riflemen.[42] Across the fields of the Maryland countryside, down the North Point Road, the British army was on the march, an hour or two away, but moving towards the city. Its progress was delayed by trees that had been felled by Stricker's rear guard.

Below Fort McHenry, the British naval squadron began their offensive maneuver. At Fort Covington, Lieutenant Henry Newcomb noted in his report:

. . . At 6 A.M., 5 bomb ships and ships of war got under way & took their station in a line abreast Fort McHenry—distance 2¾ miles & 3 miles from F. Covington . . . moderate breezes from the S.E. & hazy . . .[43]

At 6:30 A.M., the bomb vessel HMS *Volcano,* equipped with 10- and 13-inch sea mortars, came too, and fired two mortar shells to check her range. The shells fell short of the fort's batteries, and she moved closer as the other support vessels maneuvered into line, forming a half-circle two miles below Fort McHenry.[44]

Behind the naval arc of the bombardment squadron HMS *Surprize,* a 50-gun frigate flying Vice Admiral Cochrane's flag, anchored astern of Cockburn's flagship, HMS *Severn.*[45] Both ships were well beyond the range of the fort's French guns. It would be these guns from the old French warship *L'Eole* that would provide Fort McHenry with a formidable defense against the British.

A mile behind the fort were the dockyards and arsenals of Fell's Point. Out of range, but in clear view of the British, were the mastheads of numerous merchant vessels and privateers. These, along with the frigate *Java,* and sloops of war *Ontario* and *Erie,* would be inviting prizes of destruction if the stronghold of the harbor defenses, Fort McHenry, could be taken.

At this moment, Sailing Master Beverly Diggs, flotilla commander of gun barge *No. 7,* received orders to take the other merchant vessels and sink them to block the channel between the Star Fort and the Lazaretto. In a deposition made years later, Commander Diggs certified that he:

> . . . took three vessels, towed them down, and sunk them agree-ably to orders; such was the haste in which they were required to perform this duty, that no time was taken or any attempts made to save any articles that might have been on board, or even to ascertain to whom the vessels belong, that at the time of sinking the third vessel by the crew of . . . Barge [*No. 7*] it was deemed proper to take an ax & after careening the vessel cut a hole in her bottom, let her right & sink. The enemy having their bomb ships moored & commencing the bombardment . . . as it was evident to all that the obstructing of the Channel was the greatest, if not the only real preservation of the City of Baltimore . . .[46]

With the assistance of the flotillamen, Diggs began deliberately to scuttle the vessels: the schooners *Packet* and *Enterprize,* the letter of marque *Father & Son,* and the *Temperance,* among others.[47] Without these to block the harbor entrance, the British squadron would have had direct access to the shipyards of Fell's Point, and, ultimately, to the city.

Several were sunk, except for the new 130-foot steamboat packet *Chesapeake*, which presented her white starboard wheelhouse with the inscription CHESAPEAKE: UNION LINE toward the British ships. Perhaps her skipper, Captain Edward Trippe, was concerned for her integral engine parts; nevertheless, for a passenger packet she proved an ample block ship.[48]

The fort commenced a brisk fire of cannonading, with many shot and shell falling among the squadron. Cochrane decided to pull back the engaging frigates and bomb ships shortly after this to a safe distance of two miles. From here, the British were able to bombard the fort, remaining out of range of the American guns.[49]

A bomb ship was capable of hurtling a 13-inch, 190-pound cast-iron spherical exploding shell two miles. The *Niles' Weekly Register* reported ". . . that at every discharge [a bomb ship] was forced two feet into the water by the force of it, thus straining every part from stem to stern."[50] From the commencement that morning, until noon, HMS *Volcano* alone had alternately expended seventy-three shells of 10- and 13-inch caliber.[51] The bomb vessels *Aetna, Volcano, Meteor, Terror,* and *Devastation* continued their fiery assault upon the harbor batteries. Several shells fell over the fort, one of which was reported to have fallen within a hundred yards of the frigate *Java* moored at Flannagain & Parson's Wharf, nearly three miles away![52]

Along the Philadelphia Road, Captain Bird's Light Dragoons were returning toward the American lines. Not far behind, in the distance, the British army came marching into view. Observing the strongly fortified American defenses, Colonel Brooke ruled out for the moment any idea of a frontal attack. Instead, he moved the army northward in an attempt to flank the American left. His movements, however, were countered by the militia brigades under Brigadier General Winder and Stricker. Rather than risk a surprise assault on his rear, Brooke marched back to his earlier position one and one-half miles in front of the American center.[53] Colonel Brooke's assessment of the American defenses was set forth later for Lord Bathurst in his official report:

. . . Baltimore is completely surrounded by strong but detached hills, on which the enemy had constructed a chain of pallisaded redoubts, connected by a small-breastwork; I have, however, reason to think, that the defense of the northward and westward of the place, were in a very unfinished state. Chinkapin-hill, which lay in front of our position, completely commands the town; this was the strongest part of the line, and here the enemy seemed most apprehensive of an attack. These works were defended, according to the best information which we could obtain, by about 15,000 men, with a large train of artillery . . .[54]

In the entrenchments behind Rodgers Bastion, Lieutenant John Harris, who had joined the U. S. Marines at Charlestown, Maryland, viewed the spectacle of war that was before him. In a letter home he wrote:

> . . . I think the handsomest sight I ever saw was during the bombardment to see the bums and rockets flying and the firing

A sketch of Rodgers Bastion, circa 1867. From Benson J. Lossing: *The Pictorial Field-Book of the War of 1812*, New York, 1868.

from our three forts . . . I could see plenty of red coats but could not get within musket shot of them . . .[55]

The weather continued to be heavily overcast. Lieutenant Henry Newcomb noted in his report at Fort Covington, "2 P.M., wind at the N.E., with heavy showers of rain."[56] At that hour, a British bomb came plummeting from its high arc over the Patapsco River. It made its fiery approach upon Fort McHenry and landed upon a 24-pound gun mounted on the southwest bastion of the fort. No one had seen it coming in the pouring rain. Lieutenant Levi Claggett was instantly killed, and four members of the crew severely injured.

Private Isaac Munroe was nearby, but miraculously received no injury in the affair. It took valuable time to repair the carriage and remount the gun. They were attempting to clear the wreckage when another shell came down upon them. Private Munroe later described the horror he witnessed:

> . . . Sergeant [John] Clemm, a young man of most amiable character, gentlemanly manners, and real courage, was killed by my side; a bomb bursting over our heads [when] a piece of the size of a dollar, two inches thick, passed through his body in a diagonal direction from his navel, and went into the ground upwards of two feet . . .[57]

Admiral Cochrane seemingly took advantage of the momentary confusion. Since 10 A.M., the fort's guns had been silent for the most part. Perhaps the bombs had taken their effect. Signal pennants flew up the halyards and the squadron weighed and came nearer, to a distance of a mile and a half below Fort McHenry.

"The bustle necessarily produced in removing the wounded and remounting the gun," Armistead reported,

> probably induced the enemy to suspect that we were in a state of confusion, as be brought three of his bomb ships to what I believed to be good striking distance.[58]

This is what the defenders had waited for. Sailing Master Rodman of the flotilla helped move the French 36-pound naval guns through the embrasures of the lower gun batteries. Private Munroe continued his account:

> . . . The moment they had taken their position, Major Armistead

mounted the parapet and ordered a battery of 24-pounders to be opened upon them and immediately after, a battery of [36-pounders] followed, and then the whole Fort let drive at them. We could see the shot strike the frigates in several instances, when every heart was gladdened, and we gave three cheers, the music playing *Yankee Doodle* . . .[59]

The cannonading could be heard for miles. The *Niles' Weekly Register* later reported that

the houses in the city were shaken to their foundations for never, perhaps from the time of invention of cannon to the present day, were the number of pieces fired with so rapid succession.[60]

At 3 P.M., several shot hit the bomb ships *Volcano* and *Devastation* and a nearby gunboat, which caused the British ships to slip their cables, hoist sail, and remove themselves out of range of the fort's guns.[61] "Finding our shot would not reach them," Private Munroe continued,

the cannonading, which was sublime and enlivening, was ordered to be closed. We then resorted to our mortars, and fired six or eight, but sorrowful to relate, they like our shot fell short, owing to their chambers not being so deep, and were reduced to the dreadful alternative, of facing by far the most tremendous bombardment ever known this enemy, without any means of returning it . . .[62]

The defenders who were not engaged took what refuge they could find, as there were no bombproof shelters for them. Earlier, the fort's powder magazine had received a direct hit, but fortunately, the bomb failed to explode.[63] The defenders found that their woolen blankets offered little cover from the pouring rain.[64] As darkness came, the city lights were ordered extinguished.

The circumstances that followed this night irreversibly affected the final stages of the battle. Colonel Arthur Brooke, with the ever-present Admiral Cockburn pressing upon him the rewards of Baltimore, decided to launch an attack on the American front at 2 A.M. the next day. For this to be successful, however, the army needed the navy to provide a diversion. Lieutenant Gleig, who was present at the meeting, related the strategy that was proposed:

. . . To assail this position, however, without the aid of the fleet, was deemed impracticable; at least our chance of success would be greatly diminished, without their co-operation. As the left of the American army extended to a fort, built upon the brink of the river, it was clear, that, could the ships be brought to bear upon that point, and the fort be silenced by their fire, that flank of the position would be turned. This once affected, there would be no difficulty in pushing a column within their works; and as soldiers entrenched always place more reliance upon the strength of their entrenchments than upon their own personal exertions, the very sight of our people on a level with them, would in all probability decide the contest . . .[65]

Colonel Brooke sent one of his officers to Admiral Cochrane with his plan. By nightfall, the courier returned with the Vice Admiral's response. Cochrane informed Brooke,

. . . that no effectual support could be given to the land force; for such was the shallowness of the river, that none except the very lightest craft could make their way within six miles of the town; and even these were stopped by vessels sunk in the channel, and other artificial bars . . .[66]

Admiral Cochrane now had serious doubts about attacking Baltimore. In an earlier message to Cockburn, he pointed out his concerns:

My Dear Admiral, It is impossible for the ships to render you any assistance, the town is so far retired within the forts. It is for Colonel Brooke to consider under such circumstances whether he has force sufficient to defeat so large a number as it is said the enemy has collected, say 20,000 strong, or even less number & to take the town without this can be done, it will be only throwing the men's lives away and prevent us from going upon other services. At any rate every considerable loss must ensue as the enemy is daily gaining strength, his loss let it be ever so great cannot be equally felt . . .[67]

Admiral Cochrane's response stated in no small words his disapproval of an attack. Cockburn, however, still supported an attack, reminding Brooke of who had command of the land forces, per Lord Bathurst's instructions.

Towards midnight, Brooke held a council of war with his field

officers. A decision had to be made shortly in order that the fleet
might be informed, if it indeed arrived in time at all. Lieutenant
Gleig expressed his own thoughts upon the matter:

> . . . Without the help of the fleet, it was evident, that adopt what
> plan of attack we could, our loss must be such as to counterbalance
> even success itself; whilst success, under existing circumstances,
> was, to say the least of it, doubtful. And even if we should
> succeed, what would be gained by it? We could not remove
> anything from Baltimore, for want of proper conveyances. Had
> the ships been able to reach the town, then, indeed, the quantity
> of booty might have repaid the survivors for their toil, and
> consoled them for the loss of their comrades; . . . Such was the
> reasoning which influenced the council of war to decide that all
> idea of storming the enemy's lines should be given up. To draw
> them from their works would require maneuvering, and maneu-
> vering requires time; but delays were all in their favor, and could
> not possibly advantage us. Every hour brought in reinforce-
> ments to their army, whereas ours had no source from which to
> recruit its losses; and it was, therefore, deemed prudent, since we
> could not fight at once, to lose no time in returning to the
> shipping . . .[68]

Colonel Brooke immediately sent his decision to Admiral
Cochrane informing him he would "order the retreat to take place
tomorrow morning and hope to be at my destination the day after
tomorrow."[69] The courier mounted his horse and dashed off into the
rainy night uncertain whether he would reach the fleet in time.

Admiral Cochrane, not knowing of Colonel Brooke's decision, proceeded with the plan of an alternate diversionary offensive on the
Ferry Branch. At 10 P.M., several barges came alongside Cochrane's
flagship to receive final instructions. The command of the twenty
flotilla barges belonged to twenty-eight-year-old Lieutenant Charles
Napier of HMS *Euryalus*, 38 guns, who had been second in command of the Potomac offensive against Alexandria. Cochrane's order
to Lieutenant Napier was to

> . . . row up close to the [western] shore until they round the
> Point of the Patapsco and proceed up that river about one or one

and a half miles. Then let them drop their grapnels and remain perfectly quiet until one o'clock [A.M.], at which hour the Bombs will open upon the fort and sky rockets will be thrown up when you will begin a regular fire directed upon the opposite side of the river, occasionally using blank cartridges only. This is intended to take off the attention of the enemy opposite to where our army is and an attack is to be made upon their lines directly at two o'clock [A.M.] . . .[70]

At 10 P.M., Lieutenant Henry Newcomb, commanding Fort Covington, noted in his report: "The enemies barges all in motion. Weather thick & hazy with frequent showers of rain."[71]

WEDNESDAY, SEPTEMBER 14

Near midnight "the ascension of a small bright spark into the sky" briefly illuminated the darkness over the Patapsco River. On board HMS *Hebrus*, Midshipman Robert Barrett observed the tumultuous cannonading as the British squadron reopened their fire upon the harbor defenses.

> . . . All this night the bombardment continued with unabated vigor; the hissing of rockets and the fiery shells glittered in the air, threatening destruction as they fell; whilst to add solemnity to this scene of devastation, the rain fell in torrents—the thunder broke in mighty peals after each successive flash of lightening, that for a moment illuminated the surrounding darkness. This was the period, fast and approaching midnight, selected for the boats of the squadron to make a diversion in favour of our army . . .[72]

With muffled oars, Lieutenant Napier's flotilla made its silent approach up the Ferry Branch. However, because of the inclemency of that night, several of the barges unknowingly rowed eastward toward the American defenses at the Lazaretto. The remainder of Napier's flotilla continued westward past Fort McHenry, and came abreast within a few hundred yards of Fort Covington. Here they were to begin the diversionary attack at 1 A.M.

At Battery Babcock, the flotillamen had loaded their cannon with 18-pound shot and cannister. Their constant vigilance throughout the bombardment was shortly to be tested. Sailing Master John Webster later related the scene that unfolded before them:

. . . Very soon after we could discern small glimmering lights in different places. I was sure it must be the matches on board the barges, which at that time did not appear to be more than from two to three hundred yards off. Some of the lights were above me next to Fort Covington. As rapidly as possible, I mounted the cannon with my breast over the aprons of the guns, and examined the priming as it was raining fast. All being right, I trained the guns to suit my own views before firing . . .[73]

At Fort Covington, Lieutenant Newcomb also noticed the lights. Soon thereafter, the batteries of Forts Covington, Babcock, and Look-Out opened fire on the barges. The British soon returned with their own shot, many of which fell over the shore defenses. Lieutenant Newcomb described the action:

. . . The darkness prevented our accurately distinguishing their force. One bomb vessel was this side [of] the Point. A schooner about half way between her & F. Covington & the barges (number unknown, throwing 12, 18, & 24 shot) abreast of us. Our fire was directed at the headmost. A few broadsides checked their advance, when they concentrated nearly abreast of us & continued their attack on the batteries . . .[74]

Webster discovered that Six-Gun Battery was undermanned; he had only forty-five flotillamen. He had loaned thirty of his men to Lieutenant George Budd at the Circular Battery (Fort Look-Out), the day before. Midshipman Francis Andrews was dispatched to retrieve his lesser mates. That was the last Webster saw of him.[75] As for the loaned flotillamen, Lieutenant Budd had them working his own seven-gun battery.[76]

The British barges that had approached the Lazaretto caused alarm among the defenders there. Lieutenant Solomon Frazier, believing an attempt to land was being made, sent word to Commodore Rodgers. Rodgers immediately sent his aide, Master's Mate Robert Stockton, with a detachment of Pennsylvania Riflemen to counter the suspected landing.[77] Aware of their miscalculation, the British barges hastily withdrew to the safety of the squadron. With at least two of his barges hit, Lieutenant Napier continued as long as possible under the incessant firing from the shore batteries. For nearly two hours the combined batteries of the harbor defenses aimed their fire upon Napier's flotilla. Under the circumstances, Napier had provided as adequate a diversion as could be expected.

From the heights of Federal Hill, which offered a splendid panorama of the naval bombardment, the scene was surely one of supreme grandeur. A correspondent to the *Salem Gazette* described it best:

> . . . The attack on Fort McHenry, by nearly the whole British fleet was distinctly seen from Federal Hill, and from the tops of houses which were covered with men, women, and children. The night of Tuesday and the morning of Wednesday (til about 4 o'clock) presented the whole awful spectacle of shot and shells, and rockets, shooting and bursting through the air. The well directed fire of the little fort, under Lieutenant Budd, and the gallant seamen under his command, checked the enemy on his approach . . . The garrison was chiefly incommoded by the shells, which burst in and about the fort, whilst they had no bomb proof shelter. As the darkness increased, the awful grandeur of the scene augmented . . .[78]

As Napier's flotilla made its way back to the fleet, the land forces under Colonel Arthur Brooke were already marching away from Baltimore, down the North Point Road. Among the British frigates, transports, and ships of the line anchored in Old Roads Bay off North Point, a small American flag of truce vessel lay under guard of a detachment of Royal Marines. For the three American gentlemen and ten crew members aboard, the night had been one of uncertainty regarding the events of the bombardment. Together, they witnessed the first blush of daylight on the horizon shortly before 6 A.M.[79]

In the predawn hours, as the British barges came alongside the fleet, the rainstorm that had continued throughout the bombardment ended. Midshipman Barrett, aboard the frigate HMS *Hebrus*, witnessed the scene that fell before him:

> . . . as the morning dawned, the storm had passed away, and the heavens once more assumed the aspect of serenity and peace—whilst the twinkling stars shone bright and clear, and the tranquility of the night was broken only by the firing of the bombs, as they continued with unremitting assiduity to hurl their destructive missiles upon the foe . . .[80]

In the morning darkness of the Ferry Branch, where Napier's flotilla had penetrated, a 74-foot launch drifted aimlessly on the water. The loss incurred by the British in the Ferry Branch is unknown. The *Niles' Weekly Register* afterwards stated:

> They must have suffered excessively in this affair—two of their barges have been found sunk; and in them were yet some dead men. But what the loss really was, it is probable we shall never know.[81]

The bombardment upon Fort McHenry and the attack on Baltimore had failed.

9 ☆ ☆ ☆ ☆ ☆ ☆ ☆ ☆

A FLAG HOISTED—AN ANTHEM BORN

"Let the praise, then, if any be due, be given, not to me, who only did what I could not help doing, not to the writer, but to the inspirers of the song!"

—Francis Scott Key

On board the bomb ship *Volcano*, Wednesday, September 14, at 7:30 A.M. signal pennants flew up in answer to Vice Admiral Cochrane's order to discontinue firing upon the harbor defenses. Since the commencement of the bombardment, nearly twenty-four hours before, HMS *Volcano* alone had expended two hundred seventy-eight shells.[1]

The fluttering of pennants answering the signal of disengagement was carried throughout the squadron. By 9 A.M., the last vessel had spread her canvas sails, and made sail down the Patapsco River. Midshipman Barrett described the naval departure of the bombardment squadron:

> . . . Thus, after bombarding the forts and harbour of Baltimore for twenty-four hours, the squadron of frigates weighed, without firing a shot, upon the forenoon of the 14th, and were immediately followed by the bombs and sloops of war. In truth, it was a galling spectacle for the British seamen to behold. And, as the last vessel spread her canvas to the wind, the Americans hoisted a most superb and splendid ensign on their battery, and fired at the same time a gun of defiance . . . I will proceed to state, that it was with the batteries biding us defiance—the weather scowling with a thick drizzling rain upon our proceedings—whilst our hearts and spirits were depressed in the extreme—that we retired down

the Patapsco River, with far different sensations from those we experienced on entering it . . .[2]

In the Star Fort, Major George Armistead witnessed the squadron's departure. The woolen storm flag (17 feet by 25 feet) which had flown over the fort throughout the tempestuous bombardment was now lowered. A larger national flag measuring 42 feet by 30 feet was ceremoniously raised over the fort as the morning gun was fired from the ramparts.[3] This large flag had been the result of an inquiry from Major Armistead, soon after his appointment as commander, to Major General Samuel Smith in the summer of 1813:

> We, Sir, are ready at Fort McHenry to defend Baltimore against invading by the enemy. This is to say, we are ready except that we have no suitable ensign to display over the Star Fort, and it is my desire to have a flag so large that the British will have no difficulty in seeing it from a distance.[4]

A committee was selected to wait upon Mary Pickersgill, 60 Albemarle Street, Old Town, described as a "maker of ships colours and pennants, &c."[5] The officers who visited her were Commodore Joshua Barney, Brigadier General John Stricker, and Lieutenant-Colonel William McDonald, commander of the Sixth Regiment of the Maryland Infantry. On August 19, 1813, Major Armistead received his suitable ensign, along with a storm flag of the usual proportions.[6]

Now, more than a year later, Major Armistead watched his flag of defiance hoisted over the fort in this moment of victory. The popular tune of "Yankee Doodle" was played by four young musicians in Captain Evans's company of the U. S. Corps of Artillery.[7] A correspondent to a Baltimore newspaper previously had witnessed the tune played a month earlier:

> . . . Who that has ever heard the *Reveille* played at Fort McHenry by the skillful performance of that Garrison, "ear-piercing fife and spirit stirring drum," when touched by the hand of a master? . . . Of *National Airs*, we have as yet but few; but we have two that are sufficient for our purpose—*Yankee Doodle* and *Hail Columbia*—are as soul-aspiring as ever were suitable to our present situation . . .[8]

Eight miles downriver, in the deep water anchorage of Old Roads Bay, aboard the American flag of truce vessel, thirty-five-year-old Francis Scott Key witnessed the squadron's withdrawal. Years later, Key described the emotional triumph of seeing his country's flag over the fort.

> . . . Through the clouds of the war the stars of that banner still shone in my view, and I saw the discomforted host of its assailants driven back in ignominy to their ships. Then in that hour of deliverance and joyful triumph, my heart spoke; and "Does not such a country and such defenders of their country deserve a song?" was its question . . .[9]

Key, overwhelmed by the unexpected withdrawal of the British, and inspired by Major Armistead's flag over the embattled ramparts, withdrew a letter from his pocket and began to compose a few lines of poetry. The verses were wedded to a popular tune he had used earlier in his writings, "To Anacreon in Heaven," a well-known English melody.[10]

Viewing the British departure from Hampstead Hill, Commodore Rodgers wrote a brief note to the secretary of the navy.

> The enemy has been severely drubbed—as well by his army as his navy, and is now retiring down the river after expending many tons of shot, from 1800 to 2000 shells, and at least 7 or 8 hundred rockets.[11]

At Fort Covington, Lieutenant Newcomb in concluding his official report to the commodore wrote:

> . . . They sent 12's, 18's, & 24's into the fort & even to the new works on the top of the hill, where one man was wounded. Their shell & rockets, tho they went over us did no injury . . .[12]

General Smith found soon after daybreak that the British army had departed during the night unnoticed. Colonel Brooke had left a detachment of "pickets to deceive the enemy and to follow as a rear guard."[13] General Smith consented to General Winder's request to pursue the British,

> . . . however, so completely worn out [were the troops] with continued watching, and with being exposed the greater part of

the time to very inclement weather, that it was found impracticable to do anything more than pick up a few stragglers . . .[14]

The British army encamped that night six miles from Baltimore. On the fifteenth, they resumed their line of march to North Point and commenced to reembark the troops aboard the transports. General Smith informed the War Department that Major Armistead "was taken violently ill with a chill and fever" on the evening of the fifteenth, due to his excessive duties at the fort. Therefore, Smith with Armistead's approval, prevailed upon Commodore Rodgers to take command of the garrison for a few days.[15]

In the twilight hours of Friday, September 16, the small American flag of truce vessel slowly approached the entrance to the North West Branch, and glided through the passage. Between eight and nine o'clock that evening, the sloop touched alongside Hughes Wharf at Fell's Point.[16] For Key, Colonel John Skinner, and the elderly Dr. William Beanes, their long ordeal had ended. Key took quarters for the night at the Indian Queen Hotel.[17] There he revised the rough draft of the poem he had composed earlier, adding a few lines. A night of peaceful sleep was in order for the young lawyer-poet from Georgetown.

10 ☆ ☆ ☆ ☆ ☆ ☆ ☆ ☆ ☆

BLEST WITH VICTORY AND PEACE

On the morning of September 17, having completed ship repairs and troop embarkation, the British fleet weighed anchor and made sail down the Chesapeake Bay. Vice Admiral Cochrane described the Baltimore offensive in his official dispatch for the newspapers back home as "a demonstration and reconnaissance which it was deemed advisable to make upon the City of Baltimore."[1] Cochrane privately informed Lord Melville, First Lord of the Admiralty in London, that the attack on Baltimore was "contrary to my opinion, but extremely urged by the General, to which I reluctantly consented but to preserve unanimity between the two services."[2] On September 19, Cochrane sailed his squadron for Halifax, Nova Scotia, to superintend the construction of flat-bottom boats for the planned, forthcoming attack on New Orleans.

In the days following, the defenders of Baltimore received the full approbation of their commanding officers. Brigadier General Winder complimented the militia artillery at Fort McHenry for their "firmness and composure which would have honored veterans, and prove that they were worthy to co-operate with the regulars."[3] Major General Samuel Smith's orders of the nineteenth praised the flotillamen at the Lazaretto who "kept up a brisk, and it is believed a successful fire during the hottest period of the bombardment."[4]

Commodore Rodgers was still in command of Fort McHenry on the eighteenth when word was received of the American victory against the British fleet on Lake Champlain by Commodore Thomas McDonough, and the defeat of the British army at Plattsburg, New York. At noon, by orders of General Smith, a federal salute was fired, commencing with Fort McHenry and followed by the various marine batteries in the harbor.[5] The thunderous salute no doubt could be heard down the Chesapeake throughout the British fleet.

Commodore Oliver H. Perry, although fatigued by his foray earlier on the Potomac, had recovered sufficiently to be with Rodgers during the attack on Baltimore. On the eighteenth, Perry departed Baltimore to attend to personal affairs at home in Rhode Island before resuming his duties aboard the USS *Java*.[6]

On the nineteenth, Rodgers began to sink additional merchant vessels in the Ferry Branch, and set lookout boats down the bay to ascertain the British position. He informed Smith that the garrison artificers were repairing damages sustained by the fort during the bombardment.[7] Rodgers soon was ordered to return to Philadelphia with his command, leaving Captain Robert Spence in command of the Star Fort, who was subsequently relieved by Captain Evans on the twenty-first.[8] Rodgers issued the following congratulatory "General Orders" to his personnel:

> It is with peculiar pleasure that Commodore Rogers takes this opportunity of expressing to the Officers, Seamen, and Marines who accompanied him from this station on the late Expedition to Washington and the defenses of Baltimore, the high sense he entertained of their services. The cheerfulness with which they bore fatigue and the manly firmness with which they encountered many severe privations can only be equaled by the zeal and intrepidity they evinced in every situation where they were called into action or even had the prospect of coming in contact with the enemy.[9]

The collective American victories on the Canadian frontier, together with the successful defense of Baltimore, rekindled the patriotic spirit of the nation. This spirit was reflected in a new national song that was published in a handbill by the *Baltimore American & Commercial Daily Advertiser* on September 17. A militia private, Severn Teakle, stationed at Fort McHenry, received a copy. In a letter home he stated, "We have a song composed by Mr. Key of G. Town which was presented to every individual in the Fort in a separate sheet . . ."[10] The explanation which accompanied the song is believed to have been written by Key's brother-in-law, Captain Joseph H. Nicholson, about the then-anonymous author. Entitled the "Defense of Fort McHenry," Key's poem was received with enthusiasm and acclaim. Within weeks, it was published throughout the country under the title, "The Star-Spangled Banner."

In a September 18 letter to James Monroe, commending Armistead's conduct, Captain Nicholson expressed

> trust that the noble commander Major Armistead will receive the thanks and rewards of his government . . . We were like pigeons tied by the legs to be shot at, and you would have been delighted to have seen the conduct of Armistead . . . I entreat you not to let him be neglected.[11]

Verification that Nicholson's letter had been received in Washington came on the twenty-second, when Armistead had recovered sufficiently to write his wife Louisa:

> The President promptly sent my promotion [of breveted lieutenant-colonel] with a very handsome compliment. So you see, my dear wife, all is well, at least your husband has got a name and standing that nothing but divine providence could have given him, and I pray to our Heavenly Father that we may live long to enjoy.[12]

By the twenty-fourth, Armistead was able to address his official report to James Monroe. In concluding his report, Armistead summarized the effects of the bombardment:

> . . . During the bombardment, which lasted twenty-four hours (with two slight intermissions), from the best calculations I can make, from fifteen to eighteen hundred shells were thrown by the enemy. A few of these fell short. A large proportion burst over us, throwing their fragments among us and threatening destruction. Many passed over and about four hundred fell within our works. Two public buildings were materially injured, others but slightly. I am happy to inform you (wonderful as it may appear) that our loss amounts only to four killed, and twenty-four wounded . . .[13]

Formal hostilities between the United States and Great Britain ended on Christmas Eve 1814, with the signing of the Treaty of Ghent in Belgium, restoring the status quo ante bellum. However, before it could become official, the treaty would have to be carried across the Atlantic to be ratified by the United States Congress.

Unaware of the circumstances in Europe, Vice Admiral Cochrane, realizing that peace was imminent, hoped to increase England's bargaining powers at the negotiations by striking a blow at New Orleans. Two weeks later, on January 8, 1815, Cochrane's amphibious force, under the command of Major General Edward Pakenham, who replaced Major General Robert Ross, was soundly defeated at New Orleans by General Andrew Jackson.

At Baltimore, in honor of this third American victory, Major Armistead ordered a national salute to be fired on Sunday, February 5, from the ramparts of Fort McHenry.[14] This victory hastened the U. S. Congress to ratify the treaty on February 17, thus officially ending the War of 1812.

Upon the conclusion of peace, the city of Baltimore sent to President James Madison a congratulatory address. The city received the following response:

> . . . In the varied scenes which have put to the test the constancy of the nation, Baltimore ranks among the portion most distinguished for devotion to the public cause. It has the satisfaction to reflect that it boldly and promptly espoused the resort to arms when no honorable choice remained; that it found in the courage of its citizens a rampart against the assaults of an enterprizing force; that it never wavered nor temporized with the vicissitudes of the contest; and that it had an ample share in the exertions which brought it to an honorable conclusion.[15]

Appendices

Appendix I. Muster Rolls

These muster rolls will serve, I hope, as a tribute, if in recognition only, to those officers, seamen, and marines who helped defend Baltimore in her most perilous hours. The names listed as belonging to the U. S. Navy and U. S. Marines are published here for the first time.

A.

Officers, known to have been assigned to the Baltimore station for service aboard the following vessels, who took an active part in the defense of Baltimore.

U. S. Sloop of War *Erie*

George De La Roche	Sailing Master
James Page	Surgeon
Hyde Ray	Surgeon
William Mosher	Midshipman
Otho Stattings	,,
David R. Stewart	,,
George N. Hollins	,,
George Marshall	Gunnner

U. S. Sloop of War *Ontario*

Robert Trail Spence	Master Commandant
Leonard Hall	Sailing Master
George Budd	Lieutenant

William Belt	Surgeon's Mate
James McGowan	Midshipman
Solomon Rutter	,,

USS *Java*

Oliver Hazard Perry	Captain
Edward Rutledge McCall	1st Lieutenant
George Campbell Read	,,
Samuel Hambleton	Purser
Richard Lemmon	Midshipman
Rodney Fisher	,,

B.

Officers and crew of the *Guerriere* stationed at Hampstead Hill, Fort Covington, and who assisted in the U. S. gunboats. This muster roll accounts for 325 men.

Source: USS *Guerriere*, 1813-1815, Record Group 45, National Archives.

Commanding Officer
John Rodgers

Lieutenants
John H. Claoh
Thomas Gamble
Henry S. Newcomb
Charles W. Morgan
Delaney Forrest
Edward Shubrick

Sailing Master
James Ramage

Midshipmen
George Avery
Charles S. Beverly
Abraham Biglow
Joseph Bourman
James Colter
Thomas B. Curtiss
James H. Dobbin
Robert Fields
Edward Greenwell

George Hunter
Skiffinton S. Jamison
James McDobbin
William McLean
Robert Mitchell
Walter Newcomb
Charles C. Russell
William P. Salter
Silias H. Stringham
Henry R. Warner
E. W. Whitlock

Surgeon
William Turk

Surgeon's Mates
William Burchmore
Thomas Sprague

Purser
James H. Halsey

Chaplain
Samuel Severmore

Quarter-Masters
William Bennet
Shores Berg
William Casson
Ansel Cook
John Coats
John Nelson
John Higgins
Samuel Hubbard
John P. ———
George Tompkinson
Comfort Wade
Henry Warner

Steward
Joseph Thomston

Master Armorer
John D. ———

Gunner
Ezekial Darling

Quarter-Gunners
George Alexander
Elihu Anderson
John Bennet
Samuel Brown
Hugh Hannah
James Marshall
John Pierce
George F. Smith
James Steady
Seger Stout

Gunner's Mates
Johnathan Cranmere
William Goods
Andrew Matthews
John Roses
Benjamin D. Sparhawk

Boatswains
Benjamin Goodson
John Wood, Acting

Master's Mates
Samuel Alexander
Robert Stockton
John W. Wallace

Carpenters
Peter Hemmway
John W. Holms

Cockswain
Michael Clark

Cooper
Isaac Bell

Captain's Clerk
Francis A. Bond

Sail Makers
William Campbell
John DeCloso

Cook
William Robinson

Seamen
Samuel Adams
James Anderson
Manuel Antony
John Austin
Benjamin Barnis
John Baxter
John W. Beebe
Daniel Bliss
Richard Baxby
Edward Burke
Edward Boyd
Robert Bickerton
Obadiah Bowen
John Brown
Stephen Cockran
Uriel Crowel
——— Connor
John Collins
David Craig
Peter Connor
Richard Coffill
Stephen Cole
Samuel Clark
James Cole
John Cawfield
James Curay
Jonas Crows
John Dennin
Peter Davis
Samuel G. Drowne
John Daragh
William Dixon
Archibal Denneson
Charles Douglas
Francis Elliot
Richard Elmwood
Francis Edwin
Abraham Elwell
Ebenerzer Eades

——— Frazier
William L. Freeman
Robert Fessenden
Henry Flech
John Freeman
John Fitch
John Fryer
Samuel G. Foudrey
Simeon Gage
John Green, 2nd
Hugh Gordon
John Gerrish
John Giles
James Gilbert
John Gerald
Amboy Garner
Thomas Henderson
Simeon Howland
Thomas Hill, 1st
Thomas Hill, 2nd
George Huffstidler
John Hurley
Johnathan Hall
William G. Hannaball
Abraham Heod
John Holvall
John Hogden
George Hart
John Harrison
George Herrich
John Hicks
William Hendrick
Thomas Hall
Edward Ingels
Robert Johnston
Thomas Jones
Samuel Jackson
Alexander Johnson
William Johnson
John Joseph
David Jacobs
Peter James
Thomas Jones

Benjamin Jacobs
John Jones, 2nd
Thomas Keyes
Gabriel Larforque
John Lee
Eleanor Lonon
William Simmons
William Smith
Abraham Sweet
John Smith
Aaron Sunderland
Daniel Shelcott
Benjamin Stanley
John Smith
Phineas Styles
Johnathan Sevey
Henry Steward
John Russell
Charles Smith
Moses Tillitson
Henry Twinning
William Thomas, 1st
William Thomas, 2nd
Jacob Taylor
William Triddick
Daniel Taber
Joseph Tuch
Melby Townsend
Alexander Tomly
Thomas Thompson
John Williams
Henry West
Enock Wilson
Charles Willson
Charles Williams
David York
Charles Young

Ordinary Seamen
Joseph H. Adams
——— Alderson
Robert Alexander
James Annis

David Anderson
William Allen
James Archer
James Brown
Edward Brass
William Bechill
Freeman Baker
George Boose
Thomas Blaheney
John Barry
Daniel Belding
Charles Bradley
John Burns
David Bunker
William Blair
Jacob Burgess
James Bryant
Abraham Blake
Anthony Banks
James Bevins
Henry Basler
Peter Connor
Thomas Curry
James Croney
Peter Curnid
John Cook
Thomas Campbell
Charles Carpenter
John Cardiff
William David
Isaac Depoldt
Bailey Durfee
John Dormyn
Christian Denela
Jacob Davis
John Doyle
Nathaniel Elliot
Thomas Evans
Abraham Fargo
William Ferguson
John Frazier
John Farrell
Michael Galvill

John Greaton
Joseph Gerum
John D. Grove
Joseph D. Grove
Joseph Gold
Samuel Galloway
Frederick Hart
William Hunter
Henry Hyres
William Hall
John G. Harding
James Harkness
Elias Hulett
Peter Harrenbrook
John Ingersoll
William Jackson
John Johnson
Ransom Jerrison
Azel Jaquett
Emmanuel Joseph
William Kinsey
Frederick Knapper
James D. Lindsey
John Lympriey
Amos Longwell
Elijah Loveman
Benjamin Leach
Robert Luris
Charles Manuel
Nelson Mason
Daniel McGraw
Isaac Mitchell
James Matlet
Isaac Muller
Bernard Malley
John Noel
David Nathan
Henry Nichols
Henry Niel
John Phippe
William Purdie
William Patton
James Passman

John Peters
James Peterson
William Price
James Pigott
Nicholas R——
James Robbins
Richard Robinson
Axom Randall
Thomas Rosolandsom
Charles Roundy
John Richardson
Joseph Sevinson
Benard Spence
John Simpson
Daniel Sullivan
James Storey
William Smith
Samuel Swan
David Soby
Jacob Silver
Elijah Stillman
William Smith
Leonard Seeds
Andrew Stodder
William Smith
John Smith
Matthew Stimble
John Sulkinson
Archibald Taylor
John Thomas

Richard Thompson
Charles Tuttle
George Taylor
John Thomas
Adam Tice
Jacob Tarr
John Vickery
Henry Wells
Francis Walley
John Walls
John Williams
Josiah Wiley
George Whidden
Benjamin West
John Whiting
James Watson, 2nd
Samuel Whipple
Jesse Wilson
Caleb Winship
Major Wallers

Boys

Harvey Allen
Anthony Andault
Jarret Barret
James W. Bigleg
William Bremsey
John Caloin
George Davis
Benjamin Dunn

John Grant
John Green
John Jones, 1st
George A. Leineau
George Macklin
Robert B. Mills
John Morris
Johnathan Parkinson
Phillip H. Phillips
Ebenezer Pratt
Jacob Sailor
William Saul
William Smith, 3rd
John Stoker
Stephen Thrift
George White
John Williams
Richard Wilson
A. Woodruff

Rate Unknown

Brazella Hammond
John Roberts
Philip Warner
Calvin Wetherby
Reuben Williamson

C.

A detachment of the U. S. Marines assigned to the *Guerriere*, 1813-1814.
    Source: USS *Guerriere*, 1813-1815, Record Group 45, National Archives.

Commanding Officer	*Sergeants*	*Corporals*
Joseph S. Kuhn	John C. Lawson	Stephen Austin
	John Smith	Eli Crawford
First Lieutenant	John Duffy	Garret William Allen
John Harris		

Privates

John Brewer	John P. Kipp	Brittian Slocum
John Brissett	Joseph McCool	John Smith
Henry Bell	Patrick Mullen	Andrew Tomb
Isaac E. Carty	Cornelius McDougle	Jacob Twiss
James Cummings	Daniel McEllery	Peter Weyberg
Peter Downey	Thomas McGraw	Amos Warner
William Edwards	Matthew McGinnis	George Whitney
John Gibson	John McCoy	Johnathan Wayne
John Gerry	John Norrit	Christian Walter
Edward Harrison	John Riley	Thomas Warnock
	Richard Reese	William ———

D.

A guard detachment of U. S. Marines stationed at Baltimore from June 1, 1814 to July 1, 1814.

Source: "Muster Rolls of the U. S. Marine Corps," Record Group 45, National Archives.

Sergeant

Morris Palmer

Corporals

William Sitcher
Edward Moore

Privates

Manuel Fernado
Joseph Pecost
Alexander Malone
Barth B. Farrell

John Poston
John Gismer
Elias Duper
Michael Budwin
Benjamin Joiner

E.

"A Correct Return of a Detachment of United States Marines under the command of Captain Samuel Miller, at the Battle of Bladensburg, on the 24th of August 1814," and at Baltimore under Captain Samuel Bacon.

Source: U. S. Marine Corps Historical Center, Vertical File.

Captains	*wounds received at Bladensburg*
Samuel Miller	wounded severely in arm
Alexander Sevier	wounded slightly in neck

Lieutenants

Benjamin Richardson	
William Nicholls	wounded in the leg
Charles Lord	
Edmund Brook	

Fife Major
Fernado Politer

Sergeants
Thomas Holliday .... taken and parole
James Kelly................... wounded
John McKim
———— Jones
John L. Conklin
John Ziegler
Moses Stickney

Corporals
Daniel Bradley
Wilem Bradley .... wounded in leg
William Murphy
James Mullen
Thomas Hearn
Charles Denny
John Fisher

Bugler
George Woolgar

Musicians
John Goldie
James Kale
William Farr
———— Maxwell
———— Richardson

Privates
———— Arnold
———— Abick
Dudley Avery
Timothy Battle .... wounded in left breast
Charles Bowling
———— Bryant
Louis Bazille
John Bishop
———— Black
———— Bannaiman
James Burrows .... killed

——— Campbell
——— Cullen
——— Carrigan . . . . missing, supposed to be killed
James Crane
——— Christie . . . . missing, supposed to be killed
John Degraft
Nathaniel Doars
——— Duncan
——— Davis
Patrick Davin
Alex Disconbine
Charles Dechard
Peter Dunlavy
David Dishler
Charles Foley . . . . wounded
John Gibson . . . . wounded severely, breast, leg, & arms
Elijah Grans
Johnathan Graves . . . . wounded severely
John Gasner
Francis Green
William Gregory . . . . wounded
Conrad Hook . . . . killed
Joseph Howbrey . . . . wounded
Elias Humble
George Hiest
Luke Hovey . . . . killed whilst covering to take Lt. Col.
                                  Wadsworth who received three wounds
John Hiller
Jacob Hollymand
Thomas Hutchins
——— Johnson
——— Joyce
Jacob Kraft
——— King . . . . killed
George Lownes
John Lindon . . . . missing, supposed to be killed
John Murphy
Lauchlin McNeill . . . . killed
——— Morton
Daniel McFall
James McCarty
James McKnight

———— McCaffrey
———— Morgan . . . . ———— taken prisoner
———— Nimen
———— Ofsey . . . . wounded, died
John O'Connell
Elisha Osburn . . . . wounded severely
William Osler
Lyman Potter
John Place
John B. Piquett
John Ruddock
Charles M. Ross
Samuel Randle
Walter H. Richards
Jacob Steinmetz
Samuel Stablefoot
Peter Steel
Mordecai Sansbury . . . . missing, supposed to be killed
Michael Smith . . . . wounded, loss of left arm
Samuel Schrock
John Stevens
———— Taylor
John Sims
William Seed
———— Sely
———— Stephenson
Charles Vinigan
William Weller
John Wyman
David Wiley . . . . missing, supposed to be killed
Nicholas Whitely . . . . killed
———— Walker
James Woodruff
John Vance
Daniel McElroy

Hospital, Washington   October 12, 1814.
Samuel Miller, Captain

F.

The crew of the *Ontario* who were transferred to the U. S. Chesapeake
Flotilla in the spring of 1814. Of the 120 men originally transferred by Captain
Robert Spence, only 105 are listed.

Source: "The Roll of the U. S. Sloop of War *Ontario*, R. T. Spence,
Commander," Record Group 45, National Archives.

Quarter-Masters
Peter Gordon
Thomas Lang
John Lord
Elijah Loring
John Peters

Midshipman
Richard Montgomery

Armorer
John Bisbee

Gunner's Mate
Robert Harper

Quarter-Gunners
Joseph Bailey
Thomas Burke
James Foster

Seamen
John Abbott
David Autterbridge
Alex Baxter
John Baxter
Joseph Beeze
Cornelius Boice
John Brant
Edward P. Brown
John H. Buckley
Thomas Brown, 1st
Thomas Brown, 2nd
William Brown
James Cook
John Cook

John Davidson
Thomas Davis
John Denney
Richard Dixon
Timothy Donohue
Hugh Dougherty
John Dunwoody
Zachariah Fuller
Joseph Godfrey
Henry Gray
James Harvey
Thomas Hill
James Hooper
Peter Johnson
John Martin
Michael Mattis
George Miller
John Mortimer
Dennis McAllen
Jesse Nicholson
William Norman
John Poulson
George Richardson
Richard Richardson
James Sheppard
John Smith
Charles Smith
William Stanton
Emanuel Taff
Alex Thompson
Thomas Tooley
John Tucker
Michael White
William White
William Young
Michael ———

Ordinary Seamen
Adam Bastian
Nathan Allen
James Brown
John Bulgim
Thomas Busher
George Cain
John M. Connell
George W. Currie
Joab Daniels
Peter Dutill
Hirum Doudney
Stephen Elairkin
Avery Elwell
John Grace
Joseph Henry
Samuel Holland
James Johnson
Thomas Jones
William Lovering
William Moore
James Mullinif
Pursel Newbold
John Nichols
John Orr
William Peach
Joseph Peterson
Jacob Phillips
Gabriel Roulson
John Sheppard
Frederick Sodderstack
Robert Stephenson
George Thachara
John Thompson
James Ward

Landsman
Armorill Mills

Boys
Willson Denight

Ebenezer Evans
John Parker
Phillip Holliday
Asakel Roberts

Thomas Snowday
Matthew Stockan
David Willson

G.

"Muster Roll of a Corps of Marine Artillery under the command of Captain George Stiles of the 3rd Brigade, Maryland Militia in the Service of the United States, from August 31, 1814 when last mustered to October 31, 1814."

Source: Records of the War Department, Record Group 94, National Archives.

Captain
George Stiles

First Lieutenants
Joseph Gold
Baptist Mezick

Second Lieutenants
Timothy Gardner
Joel Vickers

Third Lieutenant
Francis Blackwell

Quarter-Master
John G. Bier

Sergeants
Benjamin Weeks
David Chaytor
Paul Durkee
William Spear
Edward Wynne
Egbert Van Buren

Drummer
John Reynolds

Fifer
John Miller

Privates
Holden Allen
Rathbone Baker
Thomas B. Bennett
Field F. Bennett
John Barrar, Jr.
Henry Bolten
W. P. Barnes
Tobias J. Belt
John F. Brennan
William Brotherton
James Belt, Jr.
George Beam, Jr.
Joseph Bargan
Henry Braggen
Robert Bilup
James Bowie
John Cunningham
James Cordery
John Crane
James Curtis
Joseph Clackner
Christopher Coleman
William Cathel

John Cock
Joseph Dawson
P. Dickerson
Robert Davis
Richard A. Denny
Henry Dashiel
John Durand
Elie Despeaux
James Deale
George Ellis
James Frazier
William Furlong
Benjamin Franklin
R. W. Garretson
George Gilbert
A. P. Gregg
E. Goxdwait
John Gavet
W. H. Gardner
Louis Guarnego
Henry Grant
Samuel Gardner
Walton Gorden
R. W. Glenn
W. C. Hollis
John Hyland
John Hutson

Pliney Hamilton
John Hall
James Hughes
Robert Hancock
S. H. Habskiss
W. C. Hayes
James Johnson
T. W. Jenks
Wilson Jacobs
Daniel James
Thaddeus Jackson
George Kirk
Thomas Kuinard
Matthew Kelly
Thomas M. Lane
George Lee
John Laty
N. Myers
Daniel McNeal
George Mills
John Morrison
Joshua Mezick
Daniel Monsarrat
Hugh McElderry
D. Manadier

A. McClaskey
T. C. Morris
Solomon McCombs
Francis Neighle
Isaac Ninde
John Orrick
William Owen
Charles G. Perry
John Peterson
William Peterkin
James Philips
David Parrot
Gerald Patterson
John Prior
John Peterson, Jr.
Samuel Russell
James Ramsey
Jacob Reppard
Jacob Rozen
James Rollins
Thomas Ratier
Zachariah Rhodes
John Ross
Edward Riddle
B. B. Smith

Paul Southcomb
John Scott
Samuel Shipley
Daniel Shaw
James H. Stevens
John S. Smith
William Southwait
Freeman Snow
W. A. Tucker
Perry Tilden
William Thomas
John Thompson
Joseph Thomas
James Vicker
James Weve
S. Wilkerson
David Wilson
John M. White
George Weems
William Williams, Jr.
William Wade
James Watkins
John Young
William Young
Robert Henderson

H.

"Muster Roll of a Company of Sea Fencibles, under the command of William H. Addison, in the Service of the United States, from August 31, 1814 when last mustered to October 31, 1814."

Source: Records of the War Department, Record Group 94, National Archives.

Captain
William H. Addison

Second Lieutenant
Caleb P. Robinson

Third Lieutenant
George McNeir

Boatswain
John Tyler

Gunners
Zacheous Stoker
James L. Stevens
Andrew H. Fife
Patrick Handlin
James Childs
William Peregoy

Quarter-Gunners
William Hanson
James Dawson
Samuel McDonald
Samuel Jordon
John Swift
John McCracken

Privates
Thomas Alford
Jacob Alford
John Andrews
Henry Barnhart
Lewis Barall
William Belott
Peter C. Bongers
Edward Bebee
Samuel Cook
James Crocken
George Carr
Dennis Cary
Hezekiah Cooper
James M. Clark
John Curtis
John R. Caffery
Cornelious Day
Edward Dalton
Benjamin Eliott
David Evins
William Freeman
Samuel Gardner
Ezekiel George
James George
John Gordon
Thomas B. Griffith

Samuel Hutton
John Hollings
John Harris
James Hambly
Joseph Hadley
Ephram Hands
Jacob Hane, Jr.
John Hamilton
John Ing
Joshua Izer
George Keplinger
William Lacey
Taurance Limner
Robert Mackey
Thomas McDowel
Coonrod Mestler
Alexander McCoy
John Miles
Charles McComas
John Morgan
Edward Newit
Michael Nary
William Peters
John Rook
John Rick
James Redman
Joshua Redman

Henry Shartle
Augustus Sadler
William Smith
Samuel Shryark
Richard Scott
David Skipper
Francis Sinton
Stephen Stimpson
James Simons
Luther Smithson
James Simons
Michael Shehey
Joseph Scott
John Trimble
James Vinyard
Moses Walsh
Thomas Westwood
Charles Wilson
Richard Williams
Leven W. Wood
James Wallace
William Williams
John Warrick

Servants
John Stephenson
Thomas Potter
Job Williams

I.

"Muster Roll of a Company of Sea Fencibles, under the command of Matthew S. Bunbury, in the Service of the United States, from August 31, 1814 when last mustered, to October 31, 1814."

Source: Records of the War Department, Record Group 94, National Archives.

Captain
Matthew Simmones
  Bunbury

First Lieutenant
Gregory Foy

Third Lieutenant
Gerald Gorsuch

Boatswain
James Lawrenson

Gunners
John Wood

Joseph P. White
John Valiant
Hugh Crea
George C. Wilson

Quarter-Gunners
Peter Young

Peter Goodmanson
Joseph Drear
William Wilson
Noah Higby

Privates

Charles Barbine
John Brinkman
John Brown, 1st
John Brown, 2nd
Joseph Blunt
Charles Blunt
Charles Bhare
Esma Bailey
Thomas Brown
Isaac Corderoy
John Cooper
John Craig
James Corderoy
Isaac Dear
William I. Devon
Patrick Evans
Abijah Edmunds
Elias P. Forsey

John Fletcher
Paul Frederick
Thomas Gibson
Robert Green
John Green
Anthony Green
Peter Hash
Joseph Hall
James Hanes
Adam Hayes
John Henry
John Jackson
William Jones
Myers Kincaid
Joseph Linsey
Charles Luley
Henry Manson
Martin Koog
James P. Meeks
Elias Marshall
Lewis McKnight
Archibald Montgomery
George Morris
John Oram

Jenkin Page
William Patterson
Samuel S. Ross
Joseph Rogers
William Richardson
Thomas Robertson
Timothy Stephens
Robert Sterrett
William Sparks
Alexander Smith
Lewis Tranquille
John Travlet
Richard Thompson
George Todd
Pierce Welsh
George Warfield
James Williams
Charles White
John Welsh

Servants

Aderick Smother
Pierce Reynolds
Joseph Haque

APPENDIX II. NEWCOMB'S REPORT.

The official report, dated September 18, 1814, by Lieutenant Henry S. Newcomb, commanding Fort Covington, to Commodore John Rodgers is given here for the first time. When cross-referenced with other contemporary reports concerning battle sequence, weather, and time, it provides an excellent eyewitness account by an American naval officer.

Source: John Rodgers Papers, Library of Congress.

Saturday, Sep. 10th
10 P.M. Received information that the enemy were coming up the Bay in force.

Sunday, 11th
About thirty sail now in sight. Received orders to take command of Fort Covington with a detachment of seamen. The soldiers [there] are sick with the fever & ague. At noon light airs from the S__. The headmost ships of war at anchor above Sparrows Point. The transports & smaller vessels several miles below.

Monday, 12th
Light airs from the S__ & pleasant. No visible alteration during the night. The barges & small vessels very busy thru the day. 2 P.M. The ships of war got under way & came to about 6 miles below Fort McHenry.

Tuesday, 13th
At 6 A.M. 5 Bomb ships and ships of war got under way & took their station in a line abreast Fort McHenry, distance 2¾ miles & three miles from F. Covington. 8 A.M. Moderate breezes from the S.E. & hazy. The enemy commenced the Bombardment of Fort McHenry, which was returned with shells & shot, but as they all fell short the fort discontinued firing, while the enemy continued to throw their shells with great precision & effect. 2 P.M. Wind at the N.E. with heavy showers of rain. 3 P.M. Fort McHenry recommenced firing and by taking out the coins threw the shot so well among the Bomb ships that three of them got under way & run out of gunshot & bombarded the fort more furiously than before. 10 P.M. The enemies barges all in motion. Weather thick & hazy with frequent showers of rain.

Wednesday, 14th
The enemies small vessels & barges were discovered by their lights moving up the S.W. Branch. The headmost abreast of F. Covington. Commenced firing which was immediately returned with shot, shells & rockets. Fort Babcock (or the Six Gun Battery) now opened. The darkness prevented our accurately distinguishing their force. One Bomb vessel was this side [of] the Point. A schooner about half way between her & F. Covington & the barges (number unknown, throwing 12, 18, & 24 pd. shot) abreast of us. Our fire was directed at the headmost. A few broadsides checked their advance, when they concentrated nearly abreast of us & continued their attack on the batteries. The directed superiority of our fire compelled them to retreat, when they were met by a fire from F. McHenry which, however, from the darkness of the night was soon discontinued. Col. [Griffin] Taylor's [56th] regiment of [Virginia] militia was posted in our rear. How judious his arrangement [was] I shall leave to those to say who are more competant to judge & whose duty it is to decide. The shells & rockets were thrown with little intermission till daylight, but with very little effect. The officers with me were very attentive & active. Mr. Mull _____ with you. Midshipman [George] Hunter & [Joseph]

Bourman discharged their duties assigned to them with zeal & ability. Mr. Bourman was detached to post the militia in a proper situation on our right. He discharged this duty with much judgement & returned to his guns. The seamen were extremely indignant that the enemy fought no longer.

Fort Covington   Respectfully,
September 18, 1814   H. S. Newcomb

The following brief report to Commodore John Rodgers by Lt. Henry S. Newcomb was written immediately following the bombardment on September 14, 1814.
Source: John Rodgers Papers, Library of Congress.

Wednesday Morning
Sir,
About two o'clock this morning the enemy's small craft came abreast Fort Covington, when we commenced firing & was followed by the Six Gun Battery. They soon left their station. They sent 12's 18's & 24's into the fort & even to the new works on the top of the hill, where one man was wounded. Their shell & rockets, tho they went over us did no injury.

Respectfully,
H. S. Newcomb
P.S. One of our officers was in F. McHenry about midnight—no material damage had been done. Major Armistead expressed a wish for more seamen—or rather said he thought that *thirty* seamen might be employed to great advantage in his battery.

We should like some fresh provisions & Vegetables for the men.

APPENDIX III. A LIST OF THE BRITISH NAVAL EXPEDITIONARY FLEET DURING THE BATTLE OF BALTIMORE, SEPTEMBER 12-14, 1814.

Although fifty known ships of war took part during the Baltimore campaign, because of the shallowness of the river approaches to Baltimore, most of the fleet remained at anchor off North Point in Old Roads Bay.
    Sources: British ship logs and naval correspondence. The gun rates are based on "Steele's List of the Royal Navy for 1813."

A. BOMBARDMENT SQUADRON

Bomb Ships:	*Aetna*, 8
	Devastation, 8
	Meteor, 18
	Volcano, 16
	Terror, 10
Rocket Ships:	*Erebus*, 18
Schooners:	*Seahorse*, 16
	Cockchafer, ———
	Wolverine, 18
	Rover, 18
Sloop-Brig:	*Fairy*, 12
Frigates:	*Havannah*, 36
	Hebrus, 38
	Euryalus, 36
	Severn, 36 Flagship of Rear Admiral Cockburn
	Surprize, 38 Flagship of Vice Admiral Cochrane
	Madagasgar, 38

B. NORTH POINT SQUADRON

Ships of the Line:	*Albion*, 74
	Asia, 74
	Dragon, 74
	Poictiers, 74
	Majestic, 74
	Ramilles, 74
	Royal Oak, 74 Flagship of Rear Admiral Malcolm
	Diadem, 64
	Victorious, 74
	Tonnant, 80
Schooner:	*Elizabeth*, 12
Tenders:	*Eris*
	Resolution
Sloop-Brigs:	*Manly*, 14
	Jaseur, 14
	Thistle, 20
	Tartarus, 20
	Thames, 32
Frigates:	*Belvidere*, 36
	Brune, 36
	Iphigenia, 36
	Laurestinus, 36
	Maidstone, 36

> *Diomede*, 50
> *Melpomene*, 38   Troop ship
> *Trave*, 36   Troop ship
> *Weser*, 38   Troop ship
> *Golden Fleece*, 38   Troop ship
> *Loire*, 38   Troop ship
> *Statira*, 38
> *Regulus*, 44
> *Patolus*, 36
> *Narcissus*, 32
> *Benson*, 36   Troop ship

Attached to the fleet were four divisions of troop launches. A division consisted of twenty launches and six schooners.

APPENDIX IV. BRITISH FORCES UNDER ROSS.

British forces under the command of Major General Robert Ross and the subsequent "State of a Division of the troops on the coast of North America under the command of Colonel Arthur Brooke, 44th Regiment Foot, Chesapeake, 17th September 1814."

Source: Library of Congress.

Royal Artillery	520
Royal Marine Artillery, Rocket Section	54
Royal Sappers & Miners	66
Royal Marines, 2nd & 3rd Battalions	616
4th Regiment Foot, 1st Battalion, King's Own	750
21st Regiment Foot, 1st Battalion, Royal North British Fusileers	1,117
44th Regiment Foot, 1st Battalion, East Essex	746
85th Regiment Foot, Bucks Volunteers, Light Infantry	556
Total Officers & rank & File	4,419

NOTES

For more complete information on the references cited, consult the Bibliography.

I. FORT McHENRY AND THE NATIONAL DEFENSE, 1783-1813

1. "An Act to provide a Naval Armament," March 27, 1794, *Naval Documents*, 69-70.

2. Resolution was passed by the Maryland House of Delegates on December 25, 1793, Newcomb and Thompson, 11-14.

3. Ibid.

4. "An Act to establish an Executive Department, to be denominated the Department of the Navy," April 30, 1798, *Naval Documents*, 246-47.

5. Lessem and MacKenzie, 3.

6. Ibid., 2.

7. James McHenry to John Adams, March 29, 1800, James McHenry Papers, Library of Congress (hereafter cited as LC).

8. Newcomb and Thompson, 16.

9. Ibid., 19.

10. "Acts and Resolutions of Congress," Record Group (hereafter cited as RG) 11, National Archives (hereafter cited as NA).

11. April 18, 25, 1812.

12. Adams, 314.

13. Cranwell and Crane, 46-47.

14. *Niles' Weekly Register*, August 1, 1812.

II. FORT McHENRY: SPRING, 1813

1. Byron, 21-22 (quoted from William Milbourne James, *The Naval History of Great Britain*).

2. Smith Papers, LC.

3. Levin Winder to Samuel Smith, March 13, 1813, Smith Papers, LC.

4. March 13, 1813, Smith Papers, LC.

5. Henry Dearborn to Lloyd Beall, April 9, 1812, "Letters Sent, Office of the Adjutant General," RG 107, NA. Beall's appointment to Fort McHenry also included the supervision of the military district comprehending Forts Madison and Severn in Annapolis, and Fort Washington on the Potomac.

6. Joseph Swift to Lloyd Beall, March 27, 1813, "Buell Collection of Historical Documents, U. S. Corps of Engineers," RG 77, NA. *En-barbette* are those guns set on platforms which enable them to be fired over the ramparts of a fort.

7. Lloyd Beall to John Armstrong, March 11, 1813, "Letters Received, Secretary of War, Registered Series," RG 107, NA. The *L'Eole*, commanded by Monsieur Prevost La Croix, was "driven in by stress of weather, having lost all her masts, and her rutter materially injured . . ." *American & Commercial Daily Advertizer*, September 15, 1806. In June of 1808, the *L'Eole* was put up for public auction in Baltimore. "The ships guns, gun carriages, musket shot, balls, powder, and every other war-like apparatus belonging to her . . ." were not included in the sale, Ibid., June 2, 1808.

8. Marine, 28.

9. The Committee of Public Supply was created on April 13, 1813 by Mayor Edward Johnson and members of the Baltimore City Council.

10. Samuel Smith to John Armstrong, April 21, 1813, Smith Papers, LC; Henry Miller to John Armstrong, May 9, 1813, "Letters Received, Secretary of War," RG 107, NA; John Armstrong to Henry Miller, May 1, 1813, Smith Papers, LC.

11. "Letters Received, Secretary of War," RG 107, NA.

12. Ibid., and *Niles' Weekly Register*, April 17, 1813.

13. Levin Winder to Samuel Smith, May 13, 1813, Smith Papers, LC. For further discussion see Cassell, 191-93.

14. *Niles' Weekly Register*, May 1, 1813.

15. Samuel Smith to Abrams Nicoll, May 8, 1813, Smith Papers, Columbia University (hereafter cited as CU).

16. Abrams Nicoll to Charles Gardner, May 9, 1813, "Letters Received, Office of the Adjutant General," RG 94, NA. The manual sent to Colonel David Harris was *Exercises for Garrison & Field Ordnance* (New York, 1812) by Thaddeus A. Kosciusko.

17. "Letters Received, Office of the Adjutant General," RG 94, NA.

18. Committee's Report of July 6, 1813, "Letters Received, Secretary of War," RG 107, NA.

19. John Armstrong to George Armistead, June 27, 1813, "Letters Sent, Secretary of War, Register Series," RG 107, NA.

20. George Armistead Collection, Vertical File, Fort McHenry Library.

21. "Letters Received, Secretary of War, Registered Series," RG 107, NA.

22. Decius Wadsworth to John Armstrong, May 3, 1813, "Letters Received, Secretary of War," RG 107, NA.

23. Babcock to Armstrong, December 1, 1813, "Letters Received, Secretary of War," RG 107, NA.

24. Covington received a mortal wound on November 14, 1813, after the Battle of Chrystler's Field at Williamsburg, Upper Canada, on November 11.

25. John Armstrong to George Armistead, July 27, 1813, "Letters Sent, Secretary of War," RG 107, NA.

26. John McGarry III, "Historic Furnishings Report."

27. John Armstrong to George Armistead, July 27, 1813, "Letters Sent, Secretary of War," RG 107, NA.

28. Joseph Nicholson to James Monroe, December 6, 1814, James Monroe Papers, LC.

III. FELL'S POINT RENDEZVOUS

1. Charles Gordon to Samuel Smith, April 29, 1813, Smith Papers, LC.

2. The Marine Artillery was first organized at Phamphilion's Hotel, Fell's Point in 1808. "The object of this meeting being for the immediate organization of the corps . . ." *American & Commercial Daily Advertizer*, May 19, 1808.

3. Ibid., and Joseph Gold to John Stiles, September 3, 1832, "Selected Accounts and Letters concerning the Defense of Baltimore," RG 217, NA. In the spring of 1800, George Stiles was captain of the merchant vessel *Samuel Smith* of Baltimore. In March, he encountered the French privateer *Mars*, 26 guns, and received a small engagement and escaped, *Claypoole's American Daily Advertizer*, June 30, 1800.

4. Smith Papers, LC.

5. Ibid.

6. The nine gunboats sent to Norfolk were Nos. 135-137 and Nos. 139-144.

7. Samuel Smith to William Jones, March 13, 1813, Smith Papers, LC; William Jones to Charles Gordon, March 15, 1813, "Letters Sent, Secretary of the Navy to Officers," RG 45, NA.

8. William Jones to Samuel Smith, March 14, 1813, Smith Papers, LC.

9. Decius Wadsworth to John Armstrong, May 3, 1813, "Letters Received, Secretary of War," RG 107, NA.

10. Division Orders, Samuel Smith, May 4, 1813, Smith Papers, LC.

11. Smith Papers, LC.

12. Committee of Public Supply to Thomas Galloway, July 3, 1813. War of 1812 Papers, RG 22, S1, Box 1, No. 697, Baltimore City Archives.

13. *Niles' Weekly Register*, July 27, 1813.

14. Ibid.

15. Division Orders, Samuel Smith, August 9, 1813, Smith Papers, CU.

16. Ibid., August 13, 17, 1813.

17. Samuel Smith to Peter Little, August 4, 1813, Smith Papers, LC.

18. Division Orders, Samuel Smith, August 23, 1813, Smith Papers, CU.

19. *American & Commercial Daily Advertizer*, August 25, 1813.

20. Samuel Smith to Solomon Rutter, August 30, 1813, Smith Papers, CU; Solomon Rutter to John Armstrong, October 6, 1813, "Letters Received, Adjutant General," RG 94, NA.

21. Matthew Bunbury to John Armstrong, October 4, 1813, "Letters Received, Adjutant General," RG 94, NA.

22. War of 1812 Papers, RG 22, S1, Box 1, No 559, Baltimore City Archives.

23. Chapelle, *Fulton's Steam Battery*, 141.

24. *American & Commercial Daily Advertizer*, March 3, 1814.

25. March 12, 1814, Nicholson Papers, LC.

26. Chapelle, *Fulton's Steam Battery*, 141.

27. *American & Commercial Daily Advertizer*, July 20, 1814.

28. Lieutenant Hyde had previously commanded the Marine detachment aboard the U. S. Schooner *Adeline* in March of 1813, Arthur Sinclair to William Jones, March 23, 1814, "Letters Received, Secretary of the Navy from Commanders," RG 45, NA.

29. "Letter Book, Letters Received, Commandant's Office," RG 127, NA.

30. The Thirty-Sixth and Thirty-Eighth Regiments were organized by Congress under the *Act* of January 29, 1813, *Niles' Weekly Register*, May 29, 1813.

31. Ganoe, 128.

32. *American & Commercial Daily Advertizer*, May 18, 1813.

33. Millet, 46; "Acts and Resolutions of Congress," RG 11, NA.

34. Ibid.

35. "Muster Rolls of the U. S. Marine Corps," RG 127, NA.

36. William Jones to Charles Ridgely, April 12, 1814, "Letters Sent, Secretary of the Navy to Officers," RG 45, NA.

37. "Muster Rolls of the U. S. Marine Corps," RG 127, NA.

38. Franklin Wharton to Alfred Grayson, August 4, 1814, "Letter Book, Letters Sent, Commandant's Office," RG 127, NA.

39. Cranwell and Crane, 126.

40. *Niles' Weekly Register*, February 5, 1814.

41. Bourne, 279.

42. Chapelle, *History of American Sailing Ships*, 103-4.

43. "Records of the Bureau of Naval Personnel," RG 24, NA.

44. Ibid.

45. Ibid; Cranwell and Crane, 119-20.

46. Robert Spence to William Jones, November 16, 1813, "Letters Received, Secretary of the Navy from Commanders," RG 45, NA.

47. William Jones to Edward McCall, November 23, 1813, "Letters Sent, Secretary of the Navy to Officers," RG 45, NA.

48. *American & Commercial Daily Advertizer*, May 21, 1814.

49. *Niles' Weekly Register*, February 5, 1814.

50. Ibid.

51. Ibid.

52. William Jones to Charles Ridgely, April 12, 1814, "Letters Sent, Secretary of the Navy to Officers," RG 45, NA.

53. William Jones to Robert Spence, April 7, 1814, "Letters Sent, Secretary of the Navy to Officers," RG 45, NA.

54. Strott, 261-67.

55. William Jones to Robert Spence, April 7, 1814, "Letters Sent, Secretary of the Navy to Officers," RG 45, NA.

56. Robert Spence to William Jones, February 16, 1814, "Letters Received, Secretary of the Navy from Commanders," RG 45, NA; "Muster Rolls of the U. S. Marine Corps," RG 127, NA.

57. Shomette, 19.

58. Garitee, 100.

59. Maclay, 305.

60. Barney sold his home at No. 13 South Charles Street in Baltimore in May of 1812, *American & Commercial Daily Advertizer*, May 22, 1812.

61. Manuscript Division, LC.

62. "Letters Sent, Secretary of the Navy to Officers," RG 45, NA.

63. Shomette, 24.

64. Ibid., 25-26.

65. September 2, 1813, "Letters Sent, Secretary of the Navy to Officers," RG 45, NA.

66. *Baltimore Patriot*, January 4, 1814.

67. Footner, 263.

68. Ibid.

69. Cranwell and Crane, 43-45.

70. William Jones to John Gilliard, February 1814, printed in *Niles' Weekly Register*, April 2, 1814.

71. "Acts and Resolutions of Congress," RG 11, NA.

72. Ibid; Footner, 264.

73. Footner, 264.

74. Bunbury was appointed a lieutenant in the U. S. Navy on August 4, 1798, and served on the *Montezuma*, and later commanded the U. S. Brig *Eagle* from December 1800 to June 1801. He was discharged under the Peace Establishment Act of July 20, 1801, *Naval Documents*, 22, 254, 320.

75. Tousard, 65.

76. June 18, 1813, *American State Papers*, Vol. 16, 383-84.

77. "Acts and Resolutions of Congress," RG 11, NA.

78. Matthew Bunbury to John Armstrong, Otober 4, 1813, "Letters Received, Office of the Adjutant General," RG 94, NA.

79. John Armstrong to George Armistead, February 10, 1813, "Letters Sent, Office of the Adjutant General," RG 94, NA.

80. *Niles' Weekly Register*, January 29, 1814; John Gill to John Armstrong, December 6, 1813, "Letters Received, Office of the Adjutant General," RG 94, NA.

81. John Armstrong to George Armistead, February 18, 1814, "Letters Sent, Office of the Adjutant General," RG 94, NA.

82. *Niles' Weekly Register*, January 29, 1814.

83. William Jones to Joshua Barney, February 22, 1814, "Letters Sent, Secretary of the Navy to Officers," RG 45, NA.

84. Footner, 264.

85. "Letters Received, Office of the Adjutant General," RG 94, NA; John Armstrong to Matthew Bunbury, March 7, 1814, "Letters Sent, Office of the Adjutant General," RG 94, NA.

86. John Armstrong to John Gill, March 7, 1814, "Letters Sent, Office of the Adjutant General," RG 94, NA; John Armstrong to George Armistead, March 9, 1814, "Letters Sent, Office of the Adjutant General," RG 94, NA.

87. John Armstrong to George Armistead, February 22, 1814, "Letters Sent, Office of the Adjutant General," RG 94, NA.

88. George Keyser to John Walback, February 26, 1814, "Letters Received, Office of the Adjutant General," RG 94, NA.

89. John Armstrong to John Gill, April 2, 1814, "Letters Sent, Office of the Adjutant General," RG 94, NA.

90. William Addison to John Armstrong, May 1, 1814, "Letters Received, Office of the Adjutant General," RG 94, NA; John Armstrong to William Addison, May 9, 1814, "Letters Sent, Office of the Adjutant General," RG 94, NA.

91. *American & Commercial Daily Advertizer*, June 29, 1814.

92. "Acts and Resolutions of Congress," RG 11, NA.

93. "Selected Documents, Office of the Quarter-Master Commissary General of Purchases," Entry No. 112, April 21, 1814, RG 92, NA.

94. Smith Papers, CU.

IV. SALUTES AND HUZZAS: THE USS *JAVA*

1. William Jones to James Beatty, July 26, 1814, "Letters Sent, Secretary of the Navy to Commandants and Navy Agents," RG 45, NA.

2. *Baltimore Sun*, December 20, 1861.

3. William Jones to Oliver H. Perry, July 17, 1814, "Letters Sent, Secretary of the Navy to Officers," RG 45, NA.

4. *Baltimore Patriot*, August 1, 1814.

5. August 6, 1814.

V. CONFLAGRATION AT WASHINGTON

1. Lord, 37; Admiralty to Alexander Cochrane, January 25, 1814, Cochrane Papers, LC. Sir Alexander Forrester Inglis Cochrane (1758-1832) replaced the elderly Admiral John Borlase Warren as commander in chief on April 2, 1814.

2. Robert Ross (1766-1814) was commissioned a major general on June 4, 1813.

3. "Bathurst to Commanding Officer of Troops Detached from the Mediterranean for North American Service," May 20, 1814, LC.

4. George Cockburn to Alexander Cochrane, July 17, 1814, Cochrane Papers, LC.

5. Poultney Malcolm (1768-1858) was promoted to rear admiral on December 4, 1813 and was third in command of the British naval forces.

6. William Barney to Samuel Smith, August 29, 1814, Smith Papers, LC.

7. Barrett, 457.

8. Alexander Cochrane to James Gordon, August 17, 1814, Cochrane Papers, LC. James Alexander Gordon (1782-1869) was the senior officer of the Potomac flotilla offensive against Alexandria.

9. Alexander Cochrane to Peter Parker, August 17, 1814, Cochrane Papers, LC. Sir Peter Parker (1785-1814) was mortally wounded on August 30, during an attack on Moorfields on Maryland's upper Eastern Shore; Lord, 209-10.

10. Lord, 59.

11. August 19, 1814, "Letters Sent, Secretary of the Navy to Officers," RG 45, NA.

12. *Niles' Weekly Register*, September 10, 1814.

13. David Porter to William Jones, August 23, 1814, "Area File of the Naval Records Collection," RG 45, NA.

14. John Rodgers to Joseph Kuhn, August 23, 1814, Rodgers Papers, LC. The secretary had previously ordered the first officer of the *Guerrieve*, Lieutenant Thomas Gamble to Baltimore, arriving there with a detachment on August 4, Thomas Gamble to William Jones, August 4, 1814, "Letters Received, Secretary of the Navy from Officers below the rank of Commander," RG 45, NA.

15. *Niles' Weekly Register*, August 20, 1814.

16. Barrett, 458.

17. Ibid.

18. Winder was captured at the Battle of Stoney Creek, New York on July 1, 1813, John Armstrong to William Winder, July 2, 1814, "Letters Sent, Secretary of War Relating to Military Affairs," RG 107, NA; Upton, 126.

19. Major General James Wilkerson, a contemporary officer of Winder, wrote of Winder's predicament. He "had accepted the command without means and without time to create them; he found the district without magazines or provisions or forage, without transport, tools or implements, without a commissariat or efficient quartermaster's department, without a general staff, and finally without troops," Wilkerson, 754.

20. John Armstrong to William Winder, July 2, 1814, "Letters Sent, Secretary of War Relating to Military Affairs," RG 107, NA.

21. Ibid.

22. Lord, 60.

23. William Jones to Franklin Wharton, August 20, 1814, "Letters Sent, Secretary of the Navy to Commandants and Navy Agents," RG 45, NA.

24. William Jones to Joshua Barney, August 19, 20, 1814, "Letters Sent, Secretary of the Navy to Officers," RG 45, NA.

25. Ibid.

26. Lord, 62.

27. Ibid., 68.

28. Ibid.

29. Ibid., 68-69.

30. Ibid., 69-70. Benjamin Oden, a loyal supporter of the Madison administration had earlier in the spring advertised a $40 reward for a runaway slave named Frederick. Oden described him as a "bright mulatto . . . 21 years old . . . and so fair as to show freckles," and often called himself Frederick Hall. Mr. Oden learned that Frederick had enlisted as a soldier in the Thirty-Eighth U. S. Infantry commanded by Major George Keyser under the name of William Williams on the fifth of April 1814. After the war in a bounty enlistment claim contested by Oden, the government found that Oden had not "used reasonable diligence to recover and remove his slave" and therefore was not entitled to any benefits. Frederick, alias William, took part in the defense of Fort McHenry, having his "leg blown off by a cannonball," until he was admitted to the Baltimore Hospital following the bombardment. He died a month later. *American & Commercial Daily Advertizer*, July 22, 1814, *American State Papers*, Vol. 8, 532-33.

31. Lord, 72-73.

32. "Bathurst to Commanding Officer of Troops Detached from the Medditeranean for North American Service," May 20, 1814, LC.

33. William Jones to Joshua Barney, August 19, 20, 1814, "Letters Sent,

Secretary of the Navy to Officers," RG 45, NA.

34. Shomette, 179-80.

35. George Cockburn to Alexander Cochrane, August 22, 1814, Cockburn Papers, LC.

36. Shomette, 183-86.

37. Ball, 362.

38. Gleig, *A Subaltern*, 45-46.

39. Lord, 89-90, 97-98.

40. Ibid.

41. Barrett, 460-61.

42. Lord, 82.

43. Ibid., 84.

44. Joshua Barney to William Jones, August 29, 1814, printed in *Frederick Town Herald*, September 10, 1814.

45. Lord, 86-87.

46. Ibid., 97-98.

47. Ibid., 103-4.

48. Ibid., 24.

49. Ibid., 107

50. Gleig, *A Subaltern*, 66-68.

51. Printed in *Frederick Town Herald*, September 10, 1814.

52. Ball, 362.

53. Lord, 161-69.

54. Ibid., 171.

55. *Baltimore Evening Bulletin*, May 7, 1879.

56. *National Intelligencer*, August 24, 1814.

57. David Winchester to General James Winchester, August 25, 1814, Vertical File, Fort McHenry Library.

58. Samuel Smith to Levi Winder, August 16, 1814, Smith Papers, LC.

59. Hopkins, 42.

60. William Jones to John Rodgers, August 28, 1814, Rodgers Papers, LC.

VI. THE MARITIME DEFENSE OF BALTIMORE

1. Vertical File, Fort McHenry Library.

2. Hoyt, 404-5.

3. Ibid.

4. Ibid.

5. Ibid.; Lord, 209-31.

6. Lord, 231.

7. Joseph Nicholson to Mrs. Albert Gallatin, September 4, 1814, New-York Historical Society.

8. Winder Papers, Maryland Historical Society.

9. The Observatory was erected in 1797 by Captain David Porter, father

of Commodore Porter. Schwartzaur was listed as "Keeper of the Observatory, Federal Hill," *Baltimore Directory.*

10. *Baltimore Patriot,* September 24, 1814. Mr. Hall died on September 22, 1814.

11. Cranwell and Crane, 75.

12. Ibid.

13. "Abstracts of Service of Naval Officers," RG 24, NA.

14. George Douglas to Henry Wheaton, September 3, 1814, Vertical File, Fort McHenry Library.

15. Rukert, 13-14; *Maryland Gazette,* May 2, 1789.

16. William Jones to John Rodgers, September 23, 1814, "Letters Sent, Secretary of the Navy to Officers," RG 45, NA.

17. Paul Bentalou to John Armstrong, August 28, 1814, "Letters Received, Secretary of War, Registered Series," RG 107, NA.

18. John Calhoun (Baltimore Deputy Commissary) to John Armstrong, August 28, 1814, "Letters Received, Secretary of War, Registered Series," RG 107, NA.

19. Donnelly and Long, 69.

20. Grayson to Franklin Wharton, August 28, 1814, "Letters Received, Commandant's Office," RG 127, NA. According to Captain Samuel Miller's report dated October 12, 1814 (see Appendices, I, E), a total of 114 officers and enlisted men were under his command at Bladensburg. Of these, 28 were listed as wounded, killed, missing, or captured, with Miller being severely wounded in the arm at Bladensburg. In this account only 96 men were fit for duty at Baltimore. To this total we add the Havre de Grace detachment of 50 Marines under Lieutenant Joseph Kuhn, giving a total of 146 Marines. In Captain Grayson's account of 170 Marines present at Baltimore, we must add his own detachment of 24 Marines, some of which are listed under Sergeant Palmer's return of July 1814 (see Appendices, I, D).

21. *Baltimore Sun,* September 23, 1928, account by John A. Webster to Brantz Mayer, July 22, 1853.

22. General Orders, John Rodgers, August 28, 1814, Rodgers Papers, LC.

23. *Niles' Weekly Register,* August 27, 1814.

24. Letter written aboard HMS *Tonnant,* September 19, 1814, "Letters Received, Secretary of War, Registered Series," RG 107, NA.

25. Rodgers Papers, LC.

26. Ibid.

27. William Jones to John Rodgers, August 29, 1814. Rodgers Papers, LC.

28. David Porter to William Jones, September 7, 1814, printed in *Niles' Weekly Register,* October 1, 1814.

29. Ibid.

30. September 1, 1814, Smith Papers, LC.

31. Ibid.

32. Samuel Smith to John Rodgers, James Monroe, George Armistead, and the Committee of Vigilance and Safety, September 1, 1814, Smith Papers, LC.

33. Thomas Gamble to John Rodgers, September 1, 1814, Rodgers Papers, LC. "We got within three miles of Bladensburg (when) our orders were countermanded. We were ordered back to Baltimore all except one hundred that went on to Alexandria . . ." John Harris to William Harris, September 27, 1814, War of 1812 Collection, Maryland Historical Society.

34. Letter dated "Camp near Georgetown, Thursday, September 1, 1814," *New York Evening Post*, September 13, 1814.

35. John Rodgers to William Jones, September 9, 1814, Rodgers Papers, LC.

36. Ibid.; letter dated from Baltimore, September 1, 1814, *Pittsburgh Gazette*, September 15, 1814.

37. William Jones to John Rodgers, September 3, 1814, Rodgers Papers, LC.

38. John Rodgers to William Jones, September 9, 1814, Rodgers Papers, LC.

39. *National Intelligencer*, September 6, 1814.

40. John Rodgers to Robert Spence, September 1, 1814, Rodgers Papers, LC.

41. Robert Spence to John Rodgers, September 3, 1814, Rodgers Papers, LC.

42. Samuel Smith to John Rodgers, September 3, 1814, Rodgers Papers, LC.

43. William Jones to John Rodgers, Solomon Frazier, September 3, 1814, "Letters Sent, Secretary of the Navy to Officers," RG 45, NA.

44. Ibid.

45. September 7, 1814, "Letters Received, Secretary of the Navy from Commanders," RG 45, NA.

46. *Niles' Weekly Register*, September 10, 1814.

47. William Jones to David Porter, September 8, 1814, Rodgers Papers, LC.

48. Hollins, 229.

49. Mullaly, 66.

50. Ibid.

51. January 4, 1817.

52. Winder Papers, Maryland Historical Society.

53. September 10, 1814, Rodgers Papers, LC.

VII. A FLAG OF TRUCE

1. Delaplaine, 129.

2. Ibid.

3. Ibid., 137.

4. *Federal Gazette*, August 30, 1814; also see Delaplaine, 148-51.

5. Ibid.

6. Delaplaine, 149-54.

7. Ibid., 153-54.

8. Lord, 243.

9. Ibid., 245-46, 365. Lord puts Key's vessel some eight miles down-river, near Old Roads Bay; also see Robinson, 33-58.

VIII. FOUR DAYS IN SEPTEMBER

1. September 11, 1814, Smith Papers, LC.

2. September 23, 1814, printed in *Niles' Weekly Register*, October 1, 1814.

3. September 11, 1814, Rodgers Papers, LC.

4. Brainerd, 2.

5. *Baltimore Evening Bulletin*, May 7, 1879.

6. John Stricker to Samuel Smith, September 15, 1814, printed in *Niles' Weekly Register*, September 24, 1814.

7. September 11, 1814, Rodgers Papers, LC.

8. Dillon, 188.

9. George Armistead to Secretary of War, September 24, 1814, printed in *Niles' Weekly Register*, October 1, 1814.

10. Samuel Leakin to Captain Thomas Sangsten, February 20, 1843, Fort McHenry Library. Armistead listed in his official report that the Fourteenth Regiment was present. This referred only to Major Samuel Lane of the Fourteenth. No other soldier of this regiment was present, George Armistead to Samuel Smith, September 11, 1814, Smith Papers, LC.

11. John Walback to George Armistead, May 12, 1814, "Letters Sent, Office of the Adjutant General," RG 94, NA. Under the *Act* of March 30, 1814, the First, Second, and Third Regiments of Artillery were consolidated into a single corps, known as the U. S. Corps of Artillery.

12. Frederick Evans to William Duane, August 26, 1814, "Letters Received, Office of the Adjutant General," RG 94, NA.

13. *Tercentenary History of Maryland*, vol. 4: 761-62.

14. *The (Boston) Yankee*, September 30, 1814.

15. Gleig, *A Subaltern*, 112-13, 116.

16. Roche, 261-67.

17. Ibid.

18. Ibid.

19. Robert Spence to William Jones, September 26, 1814, "Letters Received, Secretary of the Navy from Officers," RG 45, NA.

20. Hollins, 229.

21. Ibid.

22. Henry Newcomb to John Rodgers, September 18, 1814, Rodgers Papers, LC.

23. *Baltimore Sun,* September 23, 1928.

24. Ibid.

25. War of 1812 Papers, No. 865, Baltimore City Archives; Lossings, 949. The only 24-pounders in Baltimore at this time belonged to the *Java.*

26. Babcock to Samuel Smith, September 3, 1814, War of 1812 Papers, Baltimore City Archives.

27. Gleig, *A Subaltern,* 116-17.

28. John Stricker to Samuel Smith, September 15, 1814, printed in *Niles' Weekly Register,* September 24, 1814.

29. Lord, 261.

30. Gleig, *A Subaltern,* 122.

31. Ibid., 122-23.

32. Gleig, *A Narrative,* 175.

33. Arthur Brooke to Lord Bathurst, September 17, 1814, printed in *Niles' Weekly Register,* December 3, 1814.

34. Ibid.

35. Gleig, *A Subaltern,* 133.

36. John Stricker to Samuel Smith, September 15, 1814, printed in *Niles' Weekly Register,* September 24, 1814.

37. Ibid.

38. George Douglass to Henry Wheaton, September 12, 1814, Vertical File, Fort McHenry Library.

39. George Armistead to Samuel Smith, September 12, 1814, Smith Papers, LC.

40. Barrett, 462.

41. September 12, 1814, Vertical File, Fort McHenry Library.

42. Bartgis Collection, MS 1913, Maryland Historical Society.

43. Henry Newcomb to John Rodgers, September 18, 1814, Rodgers Papers, LC.

44. HMS *Volcano* logbook, September 13, 1814, LC; George Armistead to Secretary of War, September 24, 1814, printed in *Niles' Weekly Register,* October 1, 1814.

45. Lord, 270.

46. Deposition of Beverly Diggs, August 9, 1832, "Selected Accounts & Letters Concerning the Defense of Baltimore, War of 1812, General Accounting Office," RG 217, NA.

47. Ibid.

48. John Rutter to Committee of Vigilance and Safety, November 30, 1814, War of 1812 Papers, Baltimore City Archives; Shannahan, 8-11.

49. George Armistead to Secretary of War, September 24, 1814, printed in *Niles' Weekly Register,* October 1, 1814.

50. *Niles' Weekly Register*, October 1, 1814.

51. HMS *Volcano* logbook, September 13, 1814, LC.

52. Sioussat, 193.

53. September 17, 1814, printed in *Niles' Weekly Register*, December 3, 1814.

54. Ibid.

55. John Harris to William Harris, September 27, 1814, War of 1812 Collection, Maryland Historical Society.

56. Henry Newcomb to John Rodgers, September 18, 1814, Rodgers Papers, LC.

57. *The (Boston) Yankee*, September 30, 1814.

58. George Armistead to Secretary of War, September 24, 1814, printed in *Niles' Weekly Register*, October 1, 1814.

59. *The (Boston) Yankee*, September 30, 1814.

60. George Armistead to Secretary of War, September 24, 1814, printed in *Niles' Weekly Register*, October 1, 1814.

61. *The (Boston) Yankee*, September 30, 1814.

62. Ibid.

63. Lord, 281.

64. Severn Teakle to Phillip Wallis, September 23, 1814, Vertical File, Fort McHenry Library.

65. Gleig, *A Narrative*, 188-89.

66. Marine, 158.

67. September 13, 1818, (9:30 A.M.), Cochrane Papers, LC.

68. Gleig, *A Narrative*, 192-93.

69. September 13, 1814, Cochrane Papers, LC.

70. Ibid.

71. Henry Newcomb to John Rodgers, September 18, 1814, Rodgers Papers, LC.

72. Barrett, 463.

73. *Baltimore Sun*, September 23, 1928.

74. Henry Newcomb to John Rodgers, September 18, 1814, Rodgers Papers, LC.

75. *Baltimore Sun*, September 23, 1928.

76. Ibid.

77. John Rodgers to William Jones, September 23, 1814, Rodgers Papers, LC.

78. *Salem (Massachusetts) Gazette*, September 27, 1814.

79. Robinson, "New Facts," 32-37.

80. Barrett, 563.

81. September 24, 1814.

IX. A FLAG HOISTED: AN ANTHEM BORN

1. HMS *Volcano*, logbook, September 14, 1814, LC.

2. Barrett, 464-65.

3. Flag Raising: "At this time our morning gun was fired, the flag hoisted, *Yankee Doodle* played . . .," Isaac Munroe to Editor, September 17, 1814, *The (Boston) Yankee*, September 30, 1814. See Sheads, 380-82 and Lord, 365. It should be realized that the accepted measurements for a garrison flag were 40 feet by 20 feet. However, the flag that flew over the Star Fort on the forenoon of the fourteenth measured in excess of 20 feet by 10 feet. Although slightly larger, such a flag (40 feet by 20 feet) was a common sight in a garrison. In 1818, Secretary of War John Calhoun approved the "Pattern flag for all Military garrisons and public arsenals not to exceed 40 feet fly and 20 feet hoist," Callender Irvine to Captain A. Steel, October 24, 1818, "General Orders & Circulars of the War Department," RG 94, NA. The original flag was officially donated to the Smithsonian Institution in 1912; also see Duane, 203.

4. Lord, 274. The original source for this letter or copies of it could not be located.

5. *Baltimore Directory.*

6. Original receipt is on display in the Star-Spangled Banner Flag House at Pratt and Albemarle streets, Baltimore.

7. *The (Boston) Yankee*, September 30, 1814. The four musicians in Captain Evans's campany were John Tillet, Samuel Lyon, William Harris, and George Shellenberg, *Citizen Soldiers*, 67.

8. *American & Commercial Daily Advertizer*, August 17, 1814.

9. Lessem and MacKenzie, 19-20.

10. Filby and Howard, 61.

11. September 14, 1814, "Letters Received, Secretary of the Navy," RG 45, NA.

12. Henry Newcomb to John Rodgers, September 14, 1814, Rodgers Papers, LC.

13. Arthur Brooke to Lord Bathurst, September 17, 1814, printed in *Niles' Weekly Register*, December 3, 1814.

14. September 19, 1814, printed in *Niles' Weekly Register*, September 24, 1814.

15. September 17, 1814, Smith Papers, LC.

16. Lord, 295.

17. Ibid.

X. BLEST WITH VICTORY AND PEACE

1. Lord, 299.

2. Ibid.

3. Division Orders, William Winder, September 15, 1814, printed in

Niles' Weekly Register, September 24, 1814.

4. Division Orders, Samuel Smith, September 19, 1814, printed in *Niles' Weekly Register*, September 24, 1814.

5. Lord, 297-98.

6. Ibid.

7. John Rodgers to William Jones, September 20, 1814, Rodgers Papers, LC.

8. John Rodgers to Samuel Smith, September 19, 1814, Rodgers Papers, LC; John Rodgers to Robert Spence, September 20, 1814, Rodgers Papers, LC.

9. General Orders, John Rodgers, September 23, 1814, Rodgers Papers, LC.

10. Severn Teakle to Phillip Wallis, September 23, 1814, Vertical File, Fort McHenry Library. Teakle was a private in Captain John Berry's Washington Artillerists who were stationed in the fort's outer batteries.

11. September 18, 1814, Nicholson Papers, LC.

12. September 22, 1814, Armistead Papers, Vertical File, Fort McHenry Library.

13. *Niles' Weekly Register*, October 1, 1814.

14. *Niles' Weekly Register*, February 11, 1815.

15. James Madison to City of Baltimore, April 22, 1815, Vertical File, Fort McHenry Library.

BIBLIOGRAPHY

I. MANUSCRIPT COLLECTIONS

Baltimore City Archives: War of 1812 Papers.

Columbia University: Samuel Smith Papers.

Fort McHenry Library: Armistead Papers, Vertical File, Historical and Archeological Research Project.

Library of Congress: Papers of Sir Alexander Cochrane, James McHenry, James Monroe, Joseph Hopper, John Rodgers, Samuel Smith.

Maryland Historical Society: War of 1812 Collection, Winder Papers.

National Archives: Acts and Resolutions of Congress, Record Group 11; Area File of the Naval Records Collection, Record Group 45; Naval Records Collection of the Office of Naval Records and Library, Record Group 45; Navy Department, General Orders and Circulars, 1798-1815, Record Group 45; Records of the Adjutant General's Office, Record Groups 94 & 407; Records of the Bureau of Naval Personnel, Record Group 24; Records of the Office of the Chief of Engineers, Record Group 77; Records of the Office of the Secretary of War, Record Group 107; Records of the U. S. Marine Corps, Record Group 127; Selected Documents, Record Group 92.

New-York Historical Society: Albert Gallatin Papers.

U. S. Marine Corps Historical Center: Vertical File.

II. PUBLISHED WORKS

Adams, Henry. *History of the United States.* Vol. 7. New York, 1930.

American & Commercial Daily Advertizer (Baltimore), 1808-1815.

American State Papers. 50 vols. Washington, D. C., 1832-1861.

Ball, Charles. *A Narrative of the Life and Adventures of Charles Ball.* Lewistown, Pennsylvania, 1836.

Baltimore Directory, 1814.

Baltimore Federal Gazette, 1812-1815.

Baltimore Patriot & Evening Advertiser, 1812-1815.

The Baltimore Sun, 1861, 1928.

Barney, Mary., ed. *Biographical Memoir of the Late Commodore Joshua Barney.* Boston, 1832.

Barrett, Robert J. "Naval Recollections," *United Service Journal,* April 1841.

Bond, Carroll T. *The Court of Appeals of Maryland, A History.* Baltimore, 1928.

Boulden, J. E. P. *The Presbyterians of Baltimore: Their Churches and Historic Graveyards.* Baltimore, 1875.

Bourchier, Lady Jane. *Memoir of the Life of Admiral Sir Edward Codrington.* London, 1873.

Bourne, Florence M. "Thomas Kemp, Shipbuilder, and his Home, Wades Point," *Maryland Historical Magazine* 49 (1954).

Brainerd, Rev. Dr. Winthrop. *This is Christ's Church.* Baltimore, 1981.

Byron, Gilbert. *The War of 1812 on the Chesapeake Bay.* Baltimore, 1964.

Calderhead, William L. "Naval Innovation in Crises: War in the Chesapeake, 1813," *American Neptune* 36 (1976).

Callan, John F. *Military Laws of the United States.* Baltimore, 1858.

Cassel, Frank A. *Merchant Congressman in the Young Republic.* Madison, Wisconsin, 1971.

Chapelle, Howard I. *The History of the American Sailing Navy.* New York, 1949.

———. *The History of American Sailing Ships.* New York, 1935.

———. *Fulton's Steam Battery: Blockship and Catamaran.* Washington, D. C., 1964.

Citizen Soldiers, Baltimore, 1889.

Cranwell, John P., and Crane, William B. *Men of Marque.* New York, 1940.

Delaplaine, Edward S. *Francis Scott Key: Life and Times.* New York, 1937.

Derby and Jackson. *A Sketch of the Life of Commodore Robert F. Stockton.* New York, 1856.

Dillon, Richard. *We Have Met the Enemy.* New York, 1978.

Donnelly, Ralph W., and Long, Richard. "Captain Samuel Bacon, U.S.M.C., was a Man for all Seasons," *Marine Corps Gazette* (November 1978).

Duane, William. *A Military Dictionary.* Philadelphia, 1810.

———. *American Military Library.* Vol. 2. Philadelphia, 1809.

Filby, P. W., and Howard, Edward G. *Star-Spangled Books.* Baltimore, 1972.

Footner, Hulbert. *Sailor of Fortune: The Life and Adventures of Commodore Joshua Barney, U.S.N.* New York and London, 1940.

Frederick Town Herald, 1814.

Ganoe, William. *The History of the U. S. Army.* New York, 1942.

Garitee, Jerome R. *The Republic's Private Navy.* Connecticut, 1977.

Georgetown Federal Republican, 1814.

Gleig, George Robert. *A Subaltern in America: Comprising his Narrative of the Campaigns of the British Army at Baltimore, Washington during the Late War.* Philadelphia and London, 1833.

————. *A Narrative of the Campaigns of the British Army at Washington and New Orleans.* London, 1826.

Hamersley, Thomas. *General Register of the U. S. Navy and Marine Corps, 1782-1882.* Washington, D. C., 1889.

Heitman, Francis., ed. *Historical Register of the U. S. Army, 1789-1889.* Washington, D. C., 1889.

Hollins, George N. "Autobiography of Commodore George Nicholas Hollins, C.S.A.," *Maryland Historical Magazine* 34 (1939).

Hopkins, Fred W. *Tom Boyle: Master Privateer.* Cambridge, Maryland, 1976.

Hoyt, William D., ed. "Civilian Defense of Baltimore, 1814-1815," *Maryland Historical Magazine* 35 (1940).

James, William Milbourne. *The Naval History of Great Britain.* London, 1837.

Lessem, Harold I., and MacKenzie, George C. *Fort McHenry National Monument and Historic Shrine.* Washington, D. C., 1954.

Lord, Walter. *The Dawn's Early Light.* New York, 1972.

Lossing, Benson J. *The Pictorial Field Book on the War of 1812.* New York, 1868.

Maclay, Edgar S. *A History of American Privateers.* New York, 1889.

Marine, William H. *The British Invasion of Maryland, 1812-1815.* (Reprint) Baltimore, 1977.

McGarry, John, III. "Historic Furnishings Report, Historical Data: Fort McHenry National Monument and Historic Shrine." Unpublished pamphlet. National Park Service, 1983.

Millet, Allan R. *Semper Fidelis: The History of the United States Marine Corps.* New York, 1982.

Mullaly, Franklin E. "The Battle of Baltimore," *Maryland Historical Magazine* 54 (1959).

Naval Documents Relating to the Quasi-War Between the United States and France. Vol. 1. Washington, D. C., 1938.

Napier, Sir Charles. "Narrative of the Operations in the Potomac by the Squadron under Orders of Captain James A. Gordon in 1814," *United Service Journal* (London, 1833).

National Intelligencer, 1814.

Newcomb, Robert D., and Thompson, Erwin N. *Historic Structure Report:*

Fort McHenry Historical and Archeological Data. National Park Service, 1974.

New York Evening Post, 1814.

Niles' Weekly Register, 1812-1818.

Pittsburgh Gazette, 1814.

Robinson, Ralph. "New Light on Three Episodes of the British Invasion of Maryland in 1814," *Maryland Historical Magazine* 37 (1942).

———. "New Facts in the National Anthem Story," *Baltimore Magazine* 50 (1956).

Roche, George De La. "A Seaman's Notebook," *Maryland Historical Magazine* 42 (1947).

Rukert, Norman. *Federal Hill.* Baltimore, 1980.

Salem (Massachusetts) Gazette, 1814.

Shannahan, John H. K. *Steamboat'n Days.* Baltimore, 1930.

Sheads, Scott S. "Yankee Doodle Played": A Letter from Baltimore, 1814," *Maryland Historical Magazine* 76 (1981) 380-82.

Shomette, Donald G. *Flotilla: Battle for the Patuxent.* Solomons, Maryland, 1981.

Sioussat, Annie L. *Old Baltimore.* New York, 1931.

Spencer, Richard H., ed. *Genealogical & Memorial Encyclopedia of the State of Maryland.* Baltimore, 1919.

"Steele's List of American and Royal Navy for 1813" (original broadside in the New-York Historical Society) printed in Roscoe, Theodore, and Freeman, Fred, *Picture History of the U. S. Navy.* New York, 1956.

Strott, Howard J. "A Seaman's Notebook: The Travels of Captain George De La Roche," *Maryland Historical Magazine* 42 (1947).

Swanson, Neil H. *The Perilous Fight.* New York, 1945.

Tercentenary History of Maryland. Vol. 4. Compiled by Henry F. Powell. Baltimore, 1925.

Tousard, Louis De. *American Artillerists Companion.* Philadelphia, 1809.

Upton, Emory. *The Military Policy of the United States.* Washington, D. C., 1912.

Wilkerson, James. *Memoirs of My Own Times.* Philadelphia, 1816.

The (Boston) Yankee, 1814.

☆ ☆ ☆ ☆ ☆ ☆ ☆ ☆ ☆ ☆ ☆

INDEX

(Page references to maps or illustrations appear in italics. The names in Appendix I and Appendix III are not indexed.)